D0399166

How to Retire with Enough Money

How to Retire with Enough Money

and How to Know What Enough Is

Teresa Ghilarducci

Workman Publishing
New York

Library of Congress Cataloging-in-Publication Data
Ghilarducci, Teresa.
How to retire with enough money : and how to know what enough is /
by Teresa Ghilarducci.
     pages cm
ISBN 978-0-7611-8613-7 (alk. paper)
1. Retirement income—Planning. 2. Finance, Personal. I. Title.
HG179.G473 2015
332.024'014—dc23   2015017654

Interior design by Jean-Marc Troadec
Cover design by John Passineau
Illustrations by Craighton Berman

Workman books are available at special discounts when purchased in
bulk for premiums and sales promotions as well as for fund-raising or
educational use. Special editions or book excerpts can also be created
to specification. For details, contact the Special Sales Director at the
address below, or send an email to specialmarkets@workman.com.

Workman Publishing Co., Inc.
225 Varick Street
New York, NY 10014
workman.com

WORKMAN is a registered trademark of Workman Publishing Co., Inc.

Printed in the United States of America
First printing December 2015

10 9 8 7 6 5 4 3 2 1

This book is dedicated to my mother,
Marion Ghilarducci, and my son, **Joseph O'Rourke**,
who strive every day on both ends of my
generation to make their way and help others.

Acknowledgments

I would like to acknowledge the extraordinary debt to the people who wrote me long emails about their personal financial situations—I read them all more than once—and the adults who, despite working all day, took my economics classes at night and on Saturdays at San Francisco City College, union halls in Chicago, West Virginia, Detroit, Pittsburgh, South Bend, and churches all over the country, who taught me so much about personal responsibility and the dedication to a dignified life.

I would not have been able to do my work without the continued support and encouragement from my agent, Barney Karpfinger. My editor, Suzanne Rafer, was a gentle and firm hand making the manuscript a book. My biggest debt is to Jodi Compton, novelist and friend, who helped write the book. I've talked to my friend Chris Tiedemann about money since we were 11. I wouldn't think this way without her.

My husband, Rick McGahey, is my love and partner and helps me even when he doesn't know it.

Contents

Introduction

Welcome to the do-it-yourself system of retirement planning in America! Wait—you did know you're in a DIY system, right? On average, Social Security replaces about 40 percent of the income you earned before retiring. It's up to you to arrange the rest. Intimidated? Don't be! Planning a prosperous retirement is easy, if you follow these six simple steps:

First, predict when you and your spouse or partner will retire, be laid off, or be physically and mentally unable to keep your job.

Second, predict when you will die.

Third, save more than 7 percent of every dollar you earn, starting when you're 25. Oh, you're 55 now? Just save 30 percent of every dollar!

Fourth, earn at least 3 percent above inflation on your investments, every year. How? Find the best funds for the lowest price and optimally allocate them. Don't forget to get out just before a financial crisis, and get back in just when the crisis has bottomed out.

Fifth, do not withdraw any funds if you lose your job, have health troubles, get divorced, buy a house, or send a son or daughter to college (or bail him or her out of jail if you don't have an honor-student type of kid).

Sixth, time your retirement account withdrawals so that the last cent isn't spent until the day you die.

See, it's easy!

Of course, the truth is that it's not easy at all. The 401(k) account, which ushered in the do-it-yourself era, has been with us since 1978, and here's how it's worked out so far. As of this writing, the majority of Americans over 50 have $30,000 or less saved for retirement. A third of them have nothing saved. Forty-nine percent of middle-class Americans are on track to be living in or near poverty after they quit working. They'll have a food budget of about $5 a day.

These are sobering figures. By 2030, the last of the baby boomers will be 65. Right now, 12 percent of the population, or about 43 million people, are over age 65; by 2030, almost 73 million, more than 20 percent, will be. The population, in general, will grow, but the over-65 segment will grow faster. From now until 2030, more than 8,000 Americans will reach age 65 every day. Even if poverty rates for the elderly stay the same as they are today, the sheer numbers of elderly poor will be at record highs: more than 5 million, up from 3 million in 2010.

The bottom line: Too many people are facing a future in which they'll have to keep working indefinitely. They'll be dependent on an uncertain job market and on government programs perpetually threatened by budget cuts. They'll be living on someone else's terms.

How do I know all this? Because I've spent my professional life studying the economics of retirement. It's been my specialty as a professor of economics, first at the University of Notre Dame and now at the New School for Social Research in New York City. I also have more than 20 years of practical experience: I was a presidential appointee to the Pension Benefit Guaranty Corporation that insures traditional pensions for 40 million workers and a gubernatorial trustee of the $12 billion Indiana Public Employees Retirement Fund. I'm currently a trustee of a retiree health-care fund of more than $53 billion, which provides for just under a million employees' benefits for former steel and auto workers.

> Because I am an economist, people tell me their intimate money issues. The smartest people have fantasy-based retirement plans.

Because of my professional bona fides, friends often talk to me intimately about their finances. I'm happy to have these conversations, but what I hear worries me. Smart, educated people would rather put money into exotic and risky investments than pay off a loan that's costing them interest every day. They get their ideas about money from screaming headlines, hot tips, and overheard conversations. Or they trust their money to inadequately trained financial managers and brokers paid on commission.

Case in point: Not too long ago, a man earning well over $130,000 per year confided to me at a dinner party that he had $300,000 in assets for retirement, plus a traditional pension. This man thought he hadn't saved enough to be able to maintain his current lifestyle. I mentally estimated his mortality, knew he had Social Security, and figured that he didn't need to worry—provided he died sooner than he expected (which I thought he would, because he was a heavy smoker with a stressful work and personal life). Congratulations, sort of.

What is an annuity?

An annuity is a payment that lasts a lifetime. It pays a steady benefit each month for the rest of your life, no matter how long you live. The size of the benefit depends on the account balance. If you opt for a spousal annuity, your benefit will be lower, but if you die before your spouse, he or she will be paid benefits for the remainder of his or her life.

An early death shouldn't be anyone's first line of defense against poverty. But for too many people, it is. Many don't even have what that dinner-party guest had—a six-figure savings balance and a pension. To repeat what I said above, a majority of Americans nearing retirement age have less than $30,000 saved for retirement. And for most people, an old-fashioned pension is a thing of the past.

To put that in perspective, consider this: To retire at a standard of living similar to the one he or she has during their working lives, the average person with no other retirement plan besides Social Security will need eight times his or her annual salary in retirement accounts. What that adds up to will vary, since 90 percent of American working households live on an amount between $20,000 and $190,000 per year. For a household living on $50,000 per year, that means $400,000 in actual assets or an annuity equivalent. But a couple wanting to live on $190,000 per year starting at age 65 will need a lot more—$1.5 million.

What I said earlier is so important, I'm going to repeat it yet again: The majority of Americans have less than $30,000 saved, and a third of Americans have nothing at all, although they need approximately $160,000 (for those earning $20,000 yearly) to $1.5 million to supplement Social Security. It's an enormous shortfall. Furthermore, money for basic expenses is not all people need in retirement. They'll need to pay for the medical expenses that Medicare doesn't cover. The average middle-class American knows that—however, she estimates she needs about $47,000 for out-of-pocket medical costs in old age, when in reality, the figure is closer to $250,000. Phrased differently, a quarter of a million dollars. Sounds a lot scarier that way, doesn't it?

In light of this bleak picture, is there any hope for the average person trying to create a secure, comfortable retirement? I believe there is. In my many years of listening to friends' financial plans and giving them advice, I've had many success stories. Consider this one: One day, an English professor at Notre Dame overheard me ranting about the stock market in the lunchroom. That night, he converted all of his retirement accounts to a secure annuity (see the facing page). He thanked me four years later when he retired. That was a case of advice I didn't even realize I was giving, but it worked out well.

However, too often I've wished I could have done more to help friends and colleagues. Too often, I know they're walking away from these conversations feeling that my advice is too little, too late: They're staring down the barrel of a retirement coming up in a few short years, and they don't have nearly the savings they'll need.

Oddly enough, all this is happening while bookstore shelves are all but collapsing under the weight of financial-planning books, many of them specifically about retirement. The world is full of financial gurus, each with a special plan about what you have to do to get rich. Generally, these experts have the best of intentions, yet too frequently their books are overlong and padded with unnecessary material. Some feature complicated worksheets; others take a psycho-spiritual approach, suggesting that your outlook on life is a large part of what will make you "wealthy"; yet others fill up their 250-plus pages with definitions of stop orders and *stop limit orders* versus *plain market orders*. Unfortunately, it's hard for readers to learn anything when their eyes are glazing over.

Worst of all, many books shame the reader, suggesting that the current mess was created solely by average people who lack financial literacy and who buy venti lattes instead of carrying a Thermos to work. (As if only your thirst for gourmet coffee stands between you and a secure retirement!) Once again, it's hard for readers to open their minds to financial advice when they've been put on the defensive about how they've handled their money so far.

I saw the need for a retirement-planning book that would be accessible, free of lecturing, and, most of all, short. The friends who've asked me for advice would have politely taken a weighty book full of worksheets. They would have put it on their shelves, intending to read it "someday." But they would almost immediately read a short, simple, and direct book, one that acknowledges that retirement planning is a scary subject but explains how to get past fear to a plan.

So I wrote one.

Chapter One:

Facing the Facts.

Or, if you're not worried, you probably don't understand the situation.

hink for a moment about the last ad you saw for a mutual fund. Did it feature a fit, salt-and-pepper-haired couple in their 60s on a terrace or a boat watching the sun set? These ads aren't selling you a mutual fund, they're selling you an ideal life. "Invest with us," these advertisements say, "and this is what your future will look like."

The future that many Americans see for themselves is a little different. I know, because many kinds of people write to me at my website (see page 129). And they're afraid.

"I didn't work while my kids were young," one 59-year-old woman told me, "and after my divorce I didn't have a job for more than five years. My second husband has a pension from the city, but I don't know if it is enough. I told him we have to do something."

She's not alone in feeling this way. A lot of people realize they're in trouble. These worries can put a lot of strain on relationships. Another person wrote to me, "My wife is 64.5 and I'm 67.5. We're both retired and have a home that's paid for. We both get Social Security and have a fair amount in savings. After 41.5 years of marriage, we've learned how to discuss money and still remain reasonably calm and unemotional. I keep thinking we're rich, she's ready to go pick up soda bottles, and I suspect the reality is somewhere in between. Our two children don't need anything from us except continuing love and acceptance. My reason for writing is that I feel it's time to smell the roses, and I'd rather not fit that in while also collecting soda bottles to cash in."

Clearly, there's a lot of anxiety out there. And a lot of people are trying to take action. They're vowing to give up going out to lunch, they're reading investment advice, and they're turning to individual, boots-on-the-ground measures to rescue their retirement plans. But what many people don't realize is this: We had help getting into the current mess. And we need help getting out.

The 401(k)/IRA conundrum

Although personal responsibility is an important part of retirement planning, the looming crisis isn't all being caused by individuals who can't deny themselves electronic sports watches and designer handbags. We've been convinced that the jam we're in is our own fault. But it's not. This isn't just a personal problem, it's a national problem.

How'd that happen? I'm glad you asked.

The traditional pension used to be the dominant model in America. Why is this significant? Because a traditional pension is a defined-benefit plan, one that guarantees a fixed amount to the retiree. Here's how it works: The employee has a mandatory deduction taken from his paycheck throughout his working life, supplemented by contributions from his employer (although in some companies, the employer alone funds the pension). The money is held in a fund and invested by a professional. Then, after

IRAs vs. 401(k)s

IRAs are tax-advantaged retirement accounts for those who don't have a 401(k) or pension through work. Also, people who leave an employer often roll over the contents of their 401(k) plans into an IRA. (Roll over means to transfer funds without incurring a tax penalty.) Most experts advise against rolling over into an IRA; instead, they advise keeping your money in your previous employer's 401(k), even though you may end up with many 401(k) accounts scattered among your past employers. IRAs do not have the same fiduciary protection that 401(k) plans have, and the fees are even higher and the choices even worse than in a 401(k).

Traditional IRAs allow the employee to deduct contributions for the tax year in which they are made, and then the assets appreciate tax-free. The funds are taxed at the time of withdrawal (commonly called distributions), which the account holder is allowed to start taking at age 59.5, and must begin taking at age 70.5. The reasoning goes that income generally drops at retirement, and with lower income comes a lower tax bracket—so it's better to be taxed then, instead of during one's working years.

Roth IRAs were introduced in 1997. Roth IRAs are mainly good for individuals who expect to have a higher tax rate when they withdraw their income after age 59.5. A Roth IRA delays the tax advantage until withdrawals are made at retirement—but the contributions going into the plan are taxed.

retirement—and this is the key point—the employee is guaranteed a fixed-sum benefit for the rest of his life. The company has an obligation to send that monthly check no matter how the pension fund's investments perform. You can see why the choice of a financial professional to oversee the pension fund is a key hiring decision! If the pension plan's funds are poorly handled, the company will have to dip into other sources of money, such as profits, to pay off its obligations.

(A word about terminology here: The plan I've just described is what I usually call a traditional pension. But because the term is going to come up so often, I'm just going to use the word *pension*—so when you see it, that's what I mean.)

From the 1960s to the mid-1990s, about 75 percent of full-time American workers were covered by a pension, and it was a model that worked well for them. It gave people a guaranteed income after they stopped working. Equally important, during their careers, it allowed them to concentrate on what they did best—from building airplane engines to selling overcoats—without having to be amateur money managers in their evening and weekend hours. Finally, a not-insignificant benefit of the pension—and Social Security, as well—was that it gave retired people a reliable income, so they were able to keep spending and stimulating the economy. This was part of what made the American economy more stable in the middle of the twentieth century than it is now.

That was how retirement generally worked until the late 1970s, when an accountant noticed a provision in the tax code, implemented at the request of a large company, that allowed highly paid executives to take a tax break on deferred income. The accountant began promoting this tax provision to other companies, and the Internal Revenue Service allowed it, but only if employers allowed everyone working for the company into the plan. The idea caught on, and a new kind of retirement account was born, named for the loophole's place in the tax code—subsection 401(k).

What's important about this short history lesson is this: The 401(k) was originally supplementary in nature, a way for highly compensated executives to get a tax break on money set aside for retirement. This humbly named plan was never meant to be a replacement for traditional pensions. If it had been, it wouldn't have been given the dull name *401(k)*. It would have been called the Great American Pension Plan.

However, employers found the 401(k) plan to be cheaper than traditional plans. It was explained to the average employee this way: The 401(k) would give the employee freedom to invest retirement savings (or not invest—it isn't a mandatory program) as he or she chose (although the 401(k) managers and the possible investment vehicles would be the choice of the employer; employees have no say in these things), plus money put into a 401(k) account wouldn't be taxed until it was withdrawn at retirement age. Even better, often there would be matching funds from the company: 50 cents on the dollar (usually) on the 3 to 6 percent of pay that employees were allowed to contribute. That's free money! You can't beat free money!

The problem? Whereas a pension is a defined-benefit plan, a 401(k) is a defined-contribution plan. And a defined-contribution plan depends entirely on how much money an employee can afford to contribute—and remember, contributing is entirely voluntary—as well as the employer's match. How much is contributed, plus how well it is invested, determines how much money a 401(k) plan participant has after retirement. There is no fixed amount for the benefit, no guaranteed monthly

Pensions, 401(k) plans, and the non-covered

I n this book, you'll mostly hear me talking about the difference between defined-benefit and defined-contribution plans. But there's a third segment of the workforce whose situation is worse than those in 401(k) plans: those not covered by any retirement plan at all.

Employer sponsorship of retirement plans of any sort fell from a high of 60.5 percent in 2000 to a low of 50.9 percent in 2010 for all workers between the ages of 25 and 64. Who are the non-covered? Some of them are self-employed; others work for very small businesses. They're caterers, home health-care workers, people in small independent retail shops, or security staff. However, those in larger workplaces are affected, too: As unions have become weaker and unemployment rates have risen, workers' ability to negotiate for retirement plans has been undermined.

Unless they are exceptional savers, the non-covered will be relying on Social Security in old age, which, as noted earlier, will replace about 40 percent of pre-retirement income for middle-income people. For someone who earned pre-tax income of $118,500 or more per year, the replacement rate is 29 percent or lower. Someone making $118,500 (the earnings cap is adjusted for inflation) or more would get the maximum benefit of $33,930 per year (that was 2015's benefit, adjusted for inflation). You can see how not being in an employer-sponsored plan leads to higher rates of retirement insecurity.

check that keeps coming for the rest of one's life. When the money in the plan is gone, it's gone.

There are some inarguably nice perks to the 401(k) plan. But the employer's contribution to an employee's 401(k) is voluntary, and not all employers make one; others contribute very little. Of course, the larger problem is when employees themselves don't put any money into a 401(k). Young people earning less, and perhaps saving for a house or to start a family, might look at their paychecks and be unable to see how they could afford to put money into a 401(k). Of course, if they don't contribute at all, they get no tax break and no employer match. (And worse, no money is set aside toward retirement, a drawback that will come home to roost sooner than they think.) And the tax breaks that make these plans so attractive? They work out much better for higher earners, who can comfortably set aside the maximum contribution, thereby getting a bigger tax break and the largest possible employer match. Eighty percent of retirement account tax breaks go to the wealthiest 20 percent of taxpayers.

> The 401(k) favors top earners the most, and puts too much risk on the individual. But if offered, you should have one.

The move to 401(k) plans shifted most risk from the company to the worker, who now found himself the manager of a pension fund for one. Employees didn't ask for this change; neither did unions. The shift to 401(k) plans was spearheaded by big business, which was more than happy to relinquish responsibility for sending its retirees a fixed pension check every month. The tax break and the employer match were the spoonful of sugar that eased this bad medicine down the throats of the regular employees, for whom the 401(k) was a poor substitute for a defined-benefit plan.

Along with the 401(k), the Individual Retirement Account (IRA) rose to prominence during this time. IRAs provided a similar service to those who didn't have a 401(k) through their work, or who were leaving or changing jobs (but most 401(k) money ends up in these less-regulated Individual Retirement Accounts— see box, page 10).

If 401(k) plans offered a dangerous amount of responsibility and freedom to the individual worker, they at least limited choices in investments to the families of mutual stock and bond funds offered by the employer. But IRAs are really the Wild West, with the individual able to choose virtually any investment he or she wants. Want to be 100 percent in airline stocks? No problem!

Thus began what I like to call the do-it-yourself (or DIY) era of retirement planning. The DIY system works only if average people save voluntarily—sometimes at very high levels— and are savvy enough to find low-risk investments with low management fees. It requires people to keep their heads and not withdraw money during financial downturns or during personal or family emergencies. Thus, the theory goes, they'll retire having saved enough money to last the rest of their lives, regardless of how long that is or of the health problems they have in their final years.

To put it mildly, this hasn't happened. What would you expect if we were all asked to cut our own hair, install our own toilets, and do our own electrical wiring? A few of us would succeed at one of the three. But there'd be an awful lot of bowl haircuts, flooded bathrooms, and smoldering houses out there.

However, although 401(k) plans have problems, not having one is worse. So, if you have a 401(k), contribute the maximum amount and take steps to protect your money—I'll show you how.

Beware conflicted advisers

I f you're inadequately prepared for retirement, it's likely not entirely your fault. The money-management industry is not on the side of the average American. When companies voluntarily provided pensions, they signed up for the responsibility of sending those checks, even if it meant dipping into profits to do so. They also signed on to be fiduciaries, to manage the money solely in employees' interests. That's not the case with 401(k) plans and IRAs. The law doesn't yet require the brokers or money managers of these plan assets to be fiduciaries. They manage money in a professional manner, but they are conflicted, they further the interests of the financial institution, not you.

The sector of the financial industry that manages 401(k) plans and IRAs isn't as tightly regulated as the traditional pension-management sector is, and they employ a legion of highly paid lobbyists to keep it that way. It's a huge business: As of the end of 2014, IRAs and 401(k) plans totaled more than $7 trillion in mutual-fund assets! That's more than 40 percent of all mutual-fund assets. It's not hard to see why the money-management industry isn't on the side of the typical investor. For years, they've successfully opposed tighter regulations on fee disclosure, fiduciary responsibility, and protections against conflicts of interest.

Having said all that, do the 401(k) and the IRA necessarily have to be a disaster for you? Not at all. These accounts can help you create a secure retirement, if properly understood.

The 401(k) offers two significant advantages. First, you aren't taxed on income contributed to a 401(k), reducing your annual tax bill (you'll be taxed on your withdrawals, but for many people the later years are a more advantageous time to be taxed, because many of us are in a lower tax bracket in retirement).

Second, many employers will match your contribution at 50 cents to the dollar, up to a maximum of 6 percent of your pay. If you earn $100,000 a year, and put $6,000 a year into your 401(k), your company would add $3,000. You're also reducing your adjusted gross income—the taxable amount—by $6,000.

> **401(k)s have two great advantages: 1) contributions and earnings aren't taxed until you take the money out, and 2) sometimes employers will also contribute.**

So the 401(k) can be a major building block in your retirement, provided it's used correctly. By this I mean that you actually need to contribute to one. That might sound obvious, but a key reason 401(k) plans haven't worked on the national level is that Americans, for various reasons, have failed to put money in them consistently and at sufficient levels.

Another key point about using 401(k) plans right is that you need to protect your funds from unrewarding risk and from being eaten up by management fees. I'll explain how to do that later, in Chapter Five.

As I noted at the beginning of this section, the retirement crisis is a national problem, and as it currently stands, the government isn't close to fixing it. For now, the stark truth is that it's up to you to pull yourself out of this hole we're all dug into.

The starting point for this needed change? It's facing the facts, although it's hard and scary to do that. I explained in the introduction that the average middle-class American believes he or she will need about $47,000 for health care in retirement, whereas the number is closer to $250,000. What's behind that roughly $200,000 disparity? Cognitive dissonance, largely.

What is cognitive dissonance, and why is it keeping me from saving?

Consider the following situation: You want to lose weight. However, your coworker has brought a plate of homemade cookies to the break room. You then encounter dissonant (conflicting) facts: *I'd love a cookie, but I'd also love to lose weight, and cookies are high in calories.* When the facts don't line up with our desires and needs, we feel mental discomfort—so we introduce more "facts" that make the dissonance go away, at least for the moment. In the case of the break-room cookies, you might solve the problem with a set of new "facts" and accompanying rationalizations: *Those cookies have oatmeal and raisins in them, which are healthful. Plus, I don't want to hurt my coworker's feelings. Therefore, I can eat one.*

Rationalization is one way people resolve cognitive dissonance: They change one side of the equation, adjusting the "facts" until they're more psychologically comfortable. Sometimes people go further, employing what's known as magical thinking: promoting an enjoyable fantasy to a near certainty. For example, a person nearing retirement with only $30,000 in his or her accounts might think, *I know, I'll invest in a wide variety of penny stocks! At least one of them has to hit, and then I'll be rich!* Penny stocks are stocks that trade at less than $5 a share, meaning that if one did increase sharply in value, a small investment could pay off big. It's like betting a small amount of money on a racehorse that goes off at 100-to-1 odds.

Unfortunately, the horse earned those odds, just like penny stocks earned their nickname: The horse is slow, and the stocks are bad. Putting your money on either isn't a plan, it's a get-rich-quick fantasy. Do I even need to add that you shouldn't count on winning the lottery, either? Both these ideas are prime examples of magical thinking.

So if you're worried, that's a positive sign: It means you haven't retreated into denial and magical thinking. You're doing something smart. You're getting real and facing facts, and that's the first step forward.

A road map to change

In the rest of this book, I'm going to help you get past your fear and create a plan. In the next chapter, I'll show you how to get a grasp on how much money you'll need at retirement, as well as how to estimate how much you're on track to have coming in.

In Chapter Three, I talk about why it's smart to delay getting Social Security until age 70, the age at which you can get full benefits. We'll also look at some of the barriers older people face when trying to stay in the workforce and talk about how to increase your chances of staying employed.

In Chapter Four, I talk about saving money—the good ideas and the bad ideas for trimming your spending.

Chapter Five is about smart investing and proper asset allocation, and the role debt should—or, more to the point, shouldn't—play in your finances.

And in Chapter Six, I discuss a subject retirement books leave completely off the table: politics. Social Security, Medicare, and Medicaid are government programs that will provide the most secure income and medical insurance for you and anyone over 65. The government is your key retirement planning partner. Being a fully engaged, savvy partner is a key fifth step in securing a good retirement for yourself and your community, as well as making sure your kids don't have to take care of you in your old age.

Chapter Two:

Bringing Your Picture into Focus.

Or, how to estimate the retirement income you need and calculate what you're likely to have.

f you've read other books about retirement planning, you're probably familiar with the concept of "the number," that magic amount you'll need to have saved for retirement. Maybe you've wondered: Is it really possible for me to come up with a dollars-and-cents figure?

The answer, tentatively, is yes. I can't give specific financial advice in a book any more than a responsible doctor would give readers specific medical advice. However, I can provide you with the guidelines you'll need to sit down with a pencil, paper, and calculator and come up with a rough estimate of the income you'll need in retirement and how much you're on track to have. The disparity between the two will tell you how much saving you've got to do.

How much income will I need?

The short answer: enough to preserve your pre-retirement standard of living. That's what economists mean when we talk about a secure retirement. Generally, people want to go on living mostly the same way they did during their working years (except without that tedious going-to-work part). They want to buy the same kinds of groceries, pursue the same hobbies, and shop for clothes at the same stores. There might be outliers: a person with a modest income who dreams about retiring to an ocean-view house with a sailboat, or a couple with a big house and an expensive lifestyle who plan to downsize and live simply in a two-bedroom house, working in the garden. But these outliers aren't the people economists are talking about when we discuss the big issues surrounding retirement. We're talking about the average person who wants to lead a life that fits into approximately the same budget.

But how do you put "pre-retirement standard of living" in dollar terms? Here's what you need to know.

If you're like most people, in retirement you'll need 70 to 80 percent of your pre-tax, pre-retirement income. If you earn $100,000 per year, you'll need $70,000 per year, at minimum, to maintain your standard of living. Personally, I'm aiming for 100 percent. But many people can live on a bit less because they won't have work expenses in retirement: commuting costs such as gasoline and bridge tolls, upkeep on a work wardrobe, the expenses of child rearing, and, of course, saving for retirement. However, some costs will increase as you age—medical expenses, for example. Ideally, though, you'll see a net drop in expenses.

An important note here: The 70 percent target assumes you'll have paid off your mortgage by the time you retire. Start making plans now to make that happen, because the numbers on this point are trending downward. In 2014, only 65 percent of older people were mortgage-free, whereas in the 1980s, more than 80 percent of seniors owned their home outright.

The biggest factor in whether you can live comfortably on 70 percent of your previous income is where you stood on the income ladder most of your life. Wealthy people who are willing to cut non-necessary expenses can get by fairly easily on 70 percent. The working poor, however, can't. They'll likely need more than 100 percent, because they have no indulgences to trim from their budget, and medical expenses increase substantially after retirement, even with insurance.

It's likely that you fall somewhere between those two extremes. That's why economists suggest that for many middle-class individuals, closer to 80 percent of pre-retirement income is approximately what's needed. That is an argument for downsizing your lifestyle now. Why? Because you're almost certainly not going to have 100 percent of your income in retirement.

> Be realistic when planning your retirement and start paring down your spending now.

In fact, if your employer doesn't offer a pension, and you're one of the one-third of middle-class Americans who has no money in a retirement account, you're likely on track to have about 40 to 50 percent of the annual income you had in your working life. In 2011, married Americans aged 55 to 64 in the bottom half of income distribution had assets of only $130,000, including their house. Those couples in the next 40 percent of income distribution, with incomes between $52,000 and $140,000 a year, had an average of $350,000 in total wealth—home equity, retirement accounts, and so on.

And married couples in the top 10 percent? I'm still worried about them. Yes, they have incomes above $140,000 per year and an average total of about $450,000 in their houses, retirement accounts, and so on. But assuming half the wealth is in their house, leaving them with $220,000 to draw down over the rest of their lives, that'll give them about $10,000 per year—which, even with Social Security, is a long way away from $140,000.

Honestly, I'm not trying to scare you into hopelessness here. It's the opposite: I hope to motivate you to fiercely pursue a solid solution to your old-age income challenge. First, we'll start with a realistic picture of the future, so you can bring your savings and your current lifestyle into line with it. Once you know you're on track to cover the bare minimum of what you'll need later, you can always save more. First, though, you need to understand a little more about where retirement income usually comes from: Social Security, a pension, and savings.

The role of Social Security

Traditionally, economists called Social Security, pensions, and personal savings the "three-legged stool" of retirement income. This isn't a good metaphor, though, since not all the legs are of equal size, as they would be on a usable stool. Social Security is the most important leg for most Americans, replacing 40 to 50 percent of pre-retirement income for middle-class individuals. Those with higher income, who earn more than $118,500 per year, will get 29 percent or less from Social Security. Low-income workers—those making less than $40,000 per year—will have about 90 percent of their income replaced by Social Security.

If you fall in the middle, getting 40 to 50 percent, that won't be enough. The rest has to come from a pension and/or your savings. But as I've already noted, fewer and fewer people have a pension nowadays. That's why individual retirement planning has become so important: It's the only thing that'll keep many

How Social Security is calculated and how delaying benefits helps

Your monthly Social Security check can vary widely, depending on the age at which you retire. You'll receive your maximum benefit at age 70, and take a penalty for collecting earlier, with the steepest cut at 62. Knowing how your Social Security benefits are calculated is critical for planning how long to work, how much to spend, and when to collect benefits. Calculating these benefits is doable and worth the effort.

You are entitled to Social Security if you accrued 40 credits. You may earn up to four credits per year, one per three-month quarter. It takes only a modest amount of earnings in those three months to earn a credit. In 2015, the minimum was $1,220. You and your employer will have to have paid Social Security taxes, or 6.2 percent each on that pay to get the credit. If you're self-employed, you earn Social Security credits the same way employees do but you have to pay the full amount: 12.4 percent.

The "primary insurance amount," or PIA, is the monthly amount you should receive at what the government defines as your "full retirement age," which ranges from 65 to 67, depending on the year in which you were born. For those born before 1937, that age was 65; between 1937 and 1960, that age is 66; after 1960, the age is 67. So the *full* retirement age is between 65 and 67. (If you hold off till age 70, you'll receive your *maximum* amount, as noted above.)

The formula is based on the average indexed monthly earnings, or AIME, in the 35 highest-earning years after age 21, up to the Social Security wage base. In 2015, that ceiling was $118,500. At retirement, if a person has worked fewer than 35 years, missing years are filled in with zeros. If they have worked more, only the highest-earning years are considered.

The AIME is divided into three segments, called bend points (adjusted each year for wage inflation), giving you the worker's PIA. For example, say you're a 67-year-old whose total indexed earnings over your 35 highest-earning years (420 months) were $2.4 million. That $2.4 million divided by 420 months gives you an AIME of $5,714 in 2015. (All multiplications have been rounded off to the nearest dollar.)

- The first bend point is $826. This is multiplied by 90 percent: $826 x 0.9= $743.
- The second bend point is $4,980. The difference between it and the first bend point is $4,154. This is multiplied by 32 percent: $4,154 x .32 = $1,329.
- The third bend point takes the results of the AIME ($5,714) and subtracts the second bend point ($4,980).
- The result is $734. This gets multiplied by 15 percent: $734 x 0.15 = $110.10.

The sum of all these amounts (rounded down to the next-lowest dime) gives you the PIA of $2,182.80.

However, the monthly benefit that you'll actually receive depends on when you begin claiming. Better yet your benefit will be increased by the amount of price inflation. It's the best deal in American pensions.

The official Social Security website, ssa.gov, has a calculator that estimates how much you'll increase or decrease your monthly check by adjusting your retirement date. When you collect largely depends on how desperately you need the money and how long you think you will live and your spouse's situation. For some people, it makes good sense to claim earlier than age 70.

people from having to scrape by on the roughly 40 percent that Social Security provides. People are going to need to supplement their income from Social Security with at least 20 to 30 percent of their pre-retirement income drawn from pensions or a retirement account.

For those who don't have a pension and haven't saved enough, or those who had to leave their career a little sooner than they expected (and most people, sadly, say they retired sooner than they intended because they were laid off, physical or mental limitations prevented them from doing their job, or a spouse's health deteriorated), a post-retirement job is increasingly the third tier of the retirement pyramid, or at least a part of the third tier. America is certainly unique in having many elderly people depend on working for "retirement" income. Note the irony: If I'm working, how is that retirement? Unfortunately, it's just a reality of life in a country that has both a crumbling employer-based retirement system and an economy that creates more low-income jobs than any other developed nation on the planet. More Americans will have to turn to a part-time, non-career-track job to make ends meet in retirement. I'll talk more about the other realities of working later in life in the next chapter.

How much income will I have?

Knowing that retirement income generally has three sources—Social Security, a pension (maybe), and savings (perhaps supplemented with a post-retirement job)—it's possible to estimate how much you'll get upon retirement from these sources—but it's not necessarily easy. Your income will be dependent on your earnings history, how your investments perform, and your savings rate. The younger you are when you do this calculation, the more likely it is that your circumstances will change over time. Even so, it's useful to get an idea of where things stand right now; you can always adjust your thinking as time passes.

Social Security: At ssa.gov, you can check your earnings history and the estimated amount of your future monthly check. Remember, though, that amount assumes that your earnings history will continue on the same trend. If you take time off from work or are laid off, your Social Security benefit will adjust downward. If you get a promotion with a sizable raise, it'll go up.

There's one more important thing you should know about your future Social Security check: Its size will vary significantly, depending on several factors. These include how old you are when you start collecting, how long you worked (you'll have to have worked at least 40 quarters, or ten years, over the course of your adult life by the time you collect), and how much you earned. In general, if you were a high earner and retired at age 70 in 2014, your Social Security benefit would be a bit more than $3,400 per month (see box, page 26).

Your pension: If you get a pension, your plan handbook will tell you how to estimate your monthly benefit. In the average pension plan, a retiree will replace 2 percent of his or her income for every year worked. A 15-year employee would replace 30 percent, a 20-year employee would get 40 percent, and so on. Your estimate, then, will depend on how long you expect to have worked for your employer when you retire. However, policies vary: You may want to ask your HR representative to help you make this approximation.

> **Estimate how much money you'll have when you stop working, being sure to consider the best and worst scenarios.**

Savings: Here I'm considering what the final balances will be on your 401(k) and IRA accounts. Your house can be part of your savings picture, especially if you're willing to sell it later in life. But for most people, the bulk of their savings is in retirement accounts, so that's what I'm concentrating on.

Your 401(k) and IRA balances at retirement will depend on how much you contribute, how well your investments perform, and how much of those returns you've lost over the years to bank and brokerage fees. It's technically possible for you to use a compounding calculator to estimate how much money you'll have accumulated in 20 or 25 years' time. But it's unwise. A compounding calculator will ask you for at least four things: the initial contribution (what you have in savings right now); your annual contribution, meaning what you earn; what you expect your raises will be; and what percentage of your earnings you will contribute each year (if you use a compounding calculator, try to be realistic); and an assumed rate of return.

The rate of return is the part that can be a problem. Why? Most compounding calculators set a rate of return that's too high, because investment fees aren't taken into account. When you use a calculator, force down the assumed rate of return to 3 percent without inflation and 5 percent with inflation. (I go a little lower, because, well, I'm an economist and I'm conservative on this issue.) These are pretty healthy targets for the growth rate in the world economy; if you decide to use a compounding calculator, use those figures no matter what the stock market's doing this year. You don't want to estimate too high a rate of return and get a false sense of security. (A side note here: I like the AARP retirement calculator, because it calculates your Social Security benefit and you can change the assumptions easily.)

Here's an example. You're 50 years old, you earn $100,000 per year, you want to retire at age 67, and you would like to achieve about the same lifestyle you have now. You have $100,000 in your IRA and plan to contribute 10 percent of your salary per year to your 401(k). Here's how the calculator and its assumed rate of return influence your plans. If you assume that you'll earn 6 percent on your original $100,000 plus the additional contributions during the rest of your career, and 3.6 percent after you retire (the lower figure reflects a more conservative investing strategy later in life), the calculator tells you that you'll have more than enough money. But if you assume 3 percent growth from the outset, it tells you you don't have enough. Your lower assumptions on growth lead you to save about 3 percent more of your salary for retirement. Hey, what's the worst that can happen? If your returns outperform these cautious assumptions, you'll have enough money to improve your lifestyle in retirement, or you'll be covered if you live a little longer!

How much can I spend in retirement?

By the day you stop working, if you're like most people, you'll need at least eight times your annual income in retirement accounts. Ten times is better. How do economists derive this figure? By assuming a 3 to 5 percent withdrawal amount each year.

A safe withdrawal amount—the amount you can take out and be assured you will not run out of money before you die—depends

The logic behind the IRS mandatory withdrawal rules

Alittle digression: I am frequently asked about the logic behind required minimum distributions (RMDs): Why do I have to withdraw my money, and why in a certain amount? Congress conducts social policy indirectly through the tax code by giving tax breaks for activities designed to meet a social purpose. The tax code redistributes tax bills among taxpayers so that people without IRAs or 401(k) plans pay higher taxes, making up for the people with them, who don't. That subsidy is a big deal (more than $140 billion per year). The IRS wants you to have enough money to live on but wants you to withdraw the money, and pay taxes on the withdrawal, when you're old. The tax breaks are not intended for fat inheritances.

According to experts Charles Ellis, Alicia Munnel, and Andrew Eschtruth in their 2014 book, *Falling Short,* an alternative to the traditional rule of thumb (the 3 to 5 percent rule) is to base withdrawals on the RMDs. The IRS's advice is based on the market and average mortality. The best advantage of these rules is that the advice is related to your age (but, of course, not your needs or your own projected longevity).

Currently, the IRS expects someone who is 70 and 6 months to live for another 27.4 years, and thus requires you to take out 1/27.4, or 3.6 percent, that year. At age 91, they assume you will live another eight years, and if you are 105, they expect you to live another four to five years, so you're required to take out 22.2 percent. The IRS stops at 105.

on your annual rate of return, which, of course, varies. As noted, 3 to 5 percent is the suggested range, because 4 percent is the average historical rate of return on a moderately safe portfolio. It's obvious that the rate of return you earn on savings and investments will have a big effect on how long your money lasts. Less obvious is what that return will be and how much it will fluctuate. There have been long periods of time when CDs and government bonds earned a decent interest rate, and periods of time when interest rates have been quite low. Ultimately, there is no such thing as a perfectly risk-free withdrawal rate. But 4 percent is a reasonable rule of thumb, and I will use it for examples in this book.

If you want to get fancy, and vary your rate as you get older, use the nifty rules from the IRS on required minimum distributions (RMDs). They have the same goals you do. The IRS doesn't want you to run out of money in retirement, but it also doesn't want you to leave tax-free money to your heirs. That's why the IRS has minimum-distribution rules for 401(k) and IRA balances— you have to withdraw funds, starting when you reach age 70.5. Those rules are a very sensible way to plan.

Let's look at an example: a 67-year-old who earned $75,000 a year. (This is pre-tax income, as will be all the numbers in my examples, unless noted otherwise.) He'll have about 35 percent of that income, or $26,250 per year, replaced by Social Security. He wants to live on 70 percent of his pre-retirement income, or $52,500. Social Security gives him half of that, so his savings will need to provide the other $26,250 a year. Thus, he'll need to have saved roughly $500,000. If he withdraws 5.25 percent yearly, that gives him $26,250.

Getting the withdrawal rate right hardly matters, though, if it can't cover the spending he'll need to do. One of the biggest money mistakes people make is to underestimate their spending. People forget that every few years they'll have to make repairs on their homes and cars, and that there will be inflation on basic items. They also might not realize that even if they have health insurance, they still have to pay for copays, premiums, and non-covered expenses. So, keeping that in mind, our 67-year-old needs to have a budget, to monitor spending needs and withdrawals on a year-by-year basis, and he'll need to make adjustments often.

Is this sustainable in the long term? That depends on how long our retiree expects to live. Dinkytown's "How long will my retirement savings last?" calculator tells us that with a conservative 3 percent rate of return on his investments, and inflation at 5 percent, he can fund 16 years and 3 months of retirement at this rate. If he lives longer, he'll be living solely on Social Security—a pretty harsh drop in income, especially that late in life.

You can see there are a lot of unknowns in play here. Might this man live longer than 16 years in retirement? Could he get a better return on his investments than 3 percent on average? Does he dare to gamble on these things? I'd vote no: Hoping for an early death or a better return isn't a retirement plan. He's better off planning to live more frugally than on 70 percent of his income.

Okay, back to your estimation process. If you'd rather calculate your retirement income in monthly terms than in annual, that's fairly easy. The Social Security Administration website already gives estimated benefits as a monthly sum, and your HR rep or plan handbook will likely do the same for a pension. As for your lifetime, lump-sum savings, they'll translate into monthly income this way: Every $24,000 will generate roughly $100 in monthly income. These two to three estimates, added together, are the monthly income you're on track to have in retirement.

Now go back to the estimate of the income you'll need to live on in retirement, that 70 percent of your current annual earnings. Divide it by 12 to get a monthly amount, and compare it with your projected monthly income. Are the two figures close to equal? If not, you can console yourself with the fact that you're not alone: Many Americans are facing a shortfall. But at least you now have a sense of the problem. That's the first step.

FACING THE UNKNOWNS: LIFE EXPECTANCY AND JOB SECURITY

The guidelines above are fairly helpful in allowing you to do the math and figure out any gap in your savings. But an important variable can throw those estimates off. It's this: How long will you be retired? This is actually two questions in one. First, when will you have to quit working? Two, how long will you live after you quit working?

You'll notice that I say "have to quit working," not "want to retire." If you're so comfortable financially that you have a choice about when to retire, that's wonderful—but if you're reading this book, that may not be the case. And in fact, my years of study into the looming crisis have made it clear to me that most Americans aren't happily considering an early retirement; they're afraid that layoffs or other circumstances will force them out of their jobs before they have adequate savings to fund a comfortable old age. So let's look at how to realistically estimate how long you can work.

Some of us are lucky and will be able to stay in our jobs as long as we please (there are university departments where even the entirety of the junior and non-tenured faculty jumping on the end of a very long crowbar couldn't dislodge a senior tenured professor). But those employment situations are rare. Ask yourself: Is your work physically demanding? Do you have to pass an annual physical to stay employed? If not, is there pressure to retire at a certain age nonetheless? If your answer to those questions is no, consider this: Is your field prone to layoffs? Is there a high incidence of burnout? Is your work psychologically stressful and subject to a high degree of supervision? The point is, you may want to work until age 67, but you have to be realistic about whether you can.

Now let's move on to life expectancy. This is where the planning process gets a little creepy: You have to estimate when you might die and when your spouse might die, but not obsess about it. (Good luck with that.) A lot of factors are in play here, but three are primary: One, do you smoke? Two, are you overweight? (Increasing evidence links excess weight to many illnesses.) Three, do you have good or bad genes?

You know the answer to the first two questions. About the third, here's a good rule of thumb: Look to your parents and grandparents. How long did they live? Did any of them die relatively young from diseases that tend to run in families?

The upshot: If you didn't inherit bad genes and you don't smoke, it's likely that you'll live into your late 80s. Might you last even longer than that? It's possible. People who make it to their late 80s have about a 20 percent chance of living about seven years longer. Health experts can't get more precise than that; life expectancy is an inexact science.

By now, you've probably noticed a recurring theme running through everything I've discussed. It's this: Life's uncertain. No matter how much careful calculating you've done and no matter what those estimations are showing you, things could change.

What's your average?

I n this book, I talk a lot about how much of your annual income you'll need in retirement and what you'll be able to replace. But no one is hired at one pay rate and stays there for the rest of their lives. So what do I mean by your "annual" pre-retirement income? The annual income you have for the last three to five years before you quit working.

You'll have to make a realistic guess about what that figure will be. If your career has reached its "cruising altitude" and you expect mostly cost-of-living raises from now on, you're probably safe in using the pay you're earning now. But if you're still fairly young and starting out, you should set the bar higher. After all, even though in old age you might want your early-20s body back, you'll probably want to live better than you did back then.

You could be laid off, you or your partner could get a chronic illness, or you could live to the age of 99. The moral of the story: You'd be wise to save beyond what your current estimates are telling you you'll need. Personally, I'm shooting to have accumulated (from saving and investment) 15 times my annual income by the time I retire, though that's ambitious.

Pass the calculator

Maybe you're not comfortable doing these kinds of back-of-the-envelope estimates yourself. Or perhaps you want to really fine-tune your projections. In either case, online calculators can be very helpful. They let you plug in numbers and estimates specific to your situation. I recommend the AARP's retirement calculator; it can be found on AARP.org. (As of this writing, the link to the calculator isn't on the home page; you'll need to click on "Work & Retirement," then on "Retirement Planning" to locate it.) The calculator will ask your age, your salary, your savings, and some questions about Social Security and the sort of lifestyle you imagine your older self having before giving you an estimate of how much money you'll need at retirement and how much you're likely to have if you continue to earn and save at your current levels.

Another source of information is dinkytown.net. This website has a funny name, but if you like calculators, you're going to be quite pleased. Dinkytown offers a variety of calculators on Social Security benefits, 401(k) plans, Roth versus traditional IRAs, and more that can help you seriously crunch the numbers you have. Of particular interest is the calculator labeled "How long will my retirement savings last?" (Users can reset the default assumptions, so do that!)

To see how all these factors play out in real-life situations, let's look at four hypothetical people approaching the end of their working lives.

CAROL AND MARK: THE AFFLUENT NON-PLANNERS

First up are Carol and Mark. Mark works in sales and earns $80,000 a year, and Carol is an estate lawyer earning about

$150,000 per year (both are pre-tax, otherwise known as gross, numbers). They have a kid just finishing college and 20 years until retirement. They have a $250,000 mortgage. Carol and Mark aren't planning for retirement; it seems far into the future, and all the money that might have gone into savings went to paying for their kid's college. But when they do think about it, they can imagine a retirement lifestyle on about $175,000 per year (adjusted for inflation), because they'll be finished paying their college bills and, they hope, their mortgage will be paid off.

What should they do? First, Mark and Carol should make sure they never take another home equity loan (yes, they did that to pay for their kid's college) and—this is really important—they should set up a payment schedule to pay off the mortgage in less than 20 years. Second, they need to live on a lot less now. They need to start saving at least 15 percent of their income—$34,000 per year.

If they're unwilling to save at all, they could plan to live later on just their Social Security, at $5,000 a month. But that's not realistic, given the drastic drop in lifestyle it'll require. Alternatively, they could save only 10 percent per year now, and one of them could work a few years longer. But that's a gamble: Their employers, their clients, the labor market, and their health all have to cooperate.

NICK: DEBTS AND OBLIGATIONS

Next, meet Nick: a working-class, hardworking guy. He's 49 years old, married, and works as a city bus driver. He's a bit young to be considering retirement, but the stress of the job and a bad back means that he wants to be able to cut back on full-time work in about ten years. He earns $50,000 a year gross, or pre-tax, and saves about 4 percent a year, or $2,000, of that income. This has given him about $25,000 in a retirement account. But Nick also has a hefty mortgage, credit-card debt, and adult children who are in and out of marriages and jobs. Helping his kids out with their expenses is one reason Nick hasn't socked more away in his retirement account.

How much will Nick and his wife need? The main question here—and it's important for Nick to answer this truthfully—is how long he can work. Realistically, he can probably continue driving a bus into his late 50s. That's not very old, but Nick's job is liable to cause him serious back injury, which could force him out of the driver's seat. He's also at risk of being laid off, unless he's in a union.

If Nick avoids health issues and layoffs, he can keep driving a few years longer, into his early 60s. But even in that case, he'll need to find another job. Why? Nick's goal is to put off collecting Social Security as long as possible, because the longer he waits, the larger his monthly check will be, and with his minimal savings, he's going to need it.

To expand a bit on Nick's situation, let's say that his wife is also working, earns about $50,000 per year as well, and will collect her own Social Security benefit. This gives Nick some breathing room; he doesn't have to worry much about her needs if he wants to retire earlier. If Nick's wife were younger and/or not earning her own income, then it'd be a no-brainer: Nick would have to delay retirement as long as possible to provide for her.

I ran the numbers on Nick's behalf. The AARP calculator tells me that Nick needs to start saving 15 percent per year and to work full-time at his current salary. If he does this, he can stop working at 65 and still maintain his standard of living. If he feels he can't increase his savings from 4 percent to 15 percent, the calculator gives Nick another option: He can work until he's 93.

Scary. But now that reality has shaken him up, Nick can do something. First, Nick needs to pay off his mortgage and credit cards. If he doesn't, those debts could grow out of hand and threaten a financially secure old age. He should pay off those debts even before he starts setting money aside in retirement accounts. Why? Because there's no investment that'll do Nick as much good as not paying interest to the bank. Consider especially his credit-card debt: The card companies are likely charging Nick about 15 percent interest. There's no investment Nick could make that has 15 percent returns, guaranteed and non-taxable (non-taxable because he's not literally "earning" the returns).

> **Save in a retirement account now, but your best investment deal is to pay off your debt!**

We'll talk more in Chapter Four about why paying off debts even before investing is such a smart idea.

A side note here: Some financial experts (I'm one of them) would advise Nick to set aside a little money toward retirement even while he's paying off his debts—just to get in the habit of saving.

Most important, given his health and low savings levels, Nick needs to plan to live on less in retirement than he does now. Why less? Isn't the point of all this to maintain one's pre-retirement standard of living?

It is, but remember that in general, the best-case scenario is that we'll have 80 percent of our prior income. So for most people, some downsizing will be necessary. Complicating the situation is the fact that many Americans are already living above their means. Like Nick. He wouldn't be in debt if he weren't spending more than he earns. That's going to make for an even ruder awakening in retirement. If Nick is wise, he'll start trimming the flab from his lifestyle now, learning how to live well on less. It'll make for a much smoother transition later.

Finally, there's one more hard thing Nick has to do: He needs to have a frank talk with his children. They simply can't depend on Mom and Dad helping them out financially anymore. Every dollar that Nick and his wife don't have to spend on their daily needs now has to go to paying off debts and saving for their future.

JENNIFER: HANDS OFF THE PORTFOLIO!

Now let's look at Jennifer. She's 57 years old and divorced, a high-end real-estate broker earning $125,000 (pre-tax) a year. In addition, Jennifer's divorce and an inheritance have given her a whopping lump sum of $500,000. She's planning to work at the same pace until age 67, saving 10 percent of her earnings, and then she'd like to maintain about the same standard of living in retirement.

Can she achieve that? With her generous net worth, solid income, good savings habits, and future Social Security benefit, Jennifer is likely to meet that goal. She'll be able to live comfortably on 70 to 80 percent of her current income, since some of her current expenses will go away. She won't have to maintain a work wardrobe, for example. And she won't be putting all those miles on her car or upgrading to a better one every couple of years (real-estate agents drive quite a bit, and they usually have high-quality cars). Almost as important, Jennifer won't be saving for retirement anymore.

However, if Jennifer's investments earn less than 3 percent annually, she may have to work longer or live on less than $87,500 per year (her 70 percent figure). Why would her return on investments fall short? A common reason is that an educated person like Jennifer, interested in her finances, might manage her retirement account too closely. She could make unwise decisions—for example, frequently buying and selling on the day's headlines—and costing herself in brokerage commissions. High investment and banking fees are the little-known thieves of savings, doing their insidious work unnoticed while everyone is focused on market ups and downs.

I talk more about fees and how they undermine savings in Chapter Five, but here's the point: Jennifer's return is 3 percent (not unheard of in a low-interest-rate environment, like the one after the recession of 2008), so if her fees and charges are the typical 2 percent, she would earn just 1 percent. Even if inflation is at a low 2 percent, Jennifer will be losing 1 percent a year! This is a common pitfall for higher-net-worth individuals like Jennifer.

PAUL: FRUGAL TO THE BONE

What about the extremely frugal? Will a penny-pinching lifestyle allow you to be comfortable in retirement regardless of your income level? To answer that, let's consider Paul. He's a 63-year-old widower and former newspaper ad salesman. Unfortunately, Paul has no savings, but he's got a few things going for him. He's in good health at present, and his house, which his wife inherited from her parents, is completely paid for. He gets about $16,000 a year from Social Security. Perhaps most important, Paul has trimmed his expenses to the bone. He never buys anything new, instead hunting garage sales and secondhand stores. He has a large vegetable garden in the backyard, and he's very handy at keeping his old car running and fixing whatever breaks around the house.

Paul's dilemma? There are expenses that, unfortunately, even extreme frugality can't stave off. Paul will have to work part-time at $20,000 a year, indefinitely, to afford things like Medicare copays, house taxes and upkeep, and groceries.

So, how ready for retirement are you? Do you just have to maintain your current course, or are you readying your mountain-climbing gear for a nearly sheer ascent? Remember that I said this plan was simple, but *simple* does not necessarily mean "easy." For some readers, like our hypothetical Nick the bus driver, there's a lot of work to do.

In the chapters ahead, I get into useful ideas for saving and investing. But first, I'm going to talk about work during your later years and about that all-important question: the age at which you should start taking your Social Security benefits.

Chapter Three:

Working.

Or, will the job market be through with you before you're through with it?

Work: It may be the biggest love-hate relationship in your life. It keeps you young; no, it's taking years off your life. You meet many of your closest friends there, yet you wish you could work from home, free from the distractions and drama of coworkers. You're thrilled to hear the words *When can you start?* but the euphoria fades once you actually start clocking in.

And of course, like many of us, you can't wait for the day when you can retire. That is, until the time comes when you're not just daydreaming, but seriously considering whether it's time to control your own time. At that point, the decision to quit working becomes as momentous as deciding what to do for a living once was for your younger self.

In this chapter I discuss the keep-working-or-retire decision, the advantages of delaying Social Security benefits, and how to maximize the chances that you'll be welcome in the workforce later in life.

Social Security: the delay that pays

Most of us have daydreamed about winning the lottery. Your fantasy probably includes quitting your job, your coworkers watching in envy and awe as you clean out your desk. Though retirement isn't as thrilling a prospect, it's still something we look forward to. Unfortunately, unless you're unusually well prepared for retirement, one of the smartest decisions you can make is to put off the day you start collecting Social Security. The government pays a maximum benefit at age 70.

I discussed this in Chapter Two. The government calculates your benefit based on a "normal retirement age" of between 65 and 67 (depending when you were born); the system takes an early-retirement deduction before then and gives you a delayed-retirement credit for every year you delay collecting between the normal retirement age and age 70. The deduction and credits depend on the year you were born. The most drastic cut comes when you collect Social Security at the earliest possible age, 62. The greatest amount in credit comes if you delay collecting until 70. Putting off collecting is a very smart decision for most people, but not everybody. If you have a shorter-than-average life expectancy and no dependents, collecting early will maximize your lifetime benefits.

Let's illustrate this by using Nick, the bus driver with a yearly income of $50,000 who we met in Chapter Two. Nick is aware that he's unlikely to keep driving much past age 60, so he'd prefer to retire and start collecting a Social Security check at 62. But if he does, he'll suffer an approximately 43 percent cut, getting a check for only $1,131. If he retires at what the government defines as normal retirement age, 67, he'll earn a benefit of $1,587. However, if he holds off until age 70, he'll get his maximum benefit of $1,984 per month.

That's obviously the best deal financially. However, it's worth noting that Nick's life expectancy could play a role in his decision about when to retire. If Nick is a smoker whose parents both died relatively young, he might tell himself that realistically, he's unlikely to live past his 70s. If Nick works until age 70, but lives only to age 78, something interesting happens to the lifetime amount he collects from Social Security: It goes down. Why? Because even though he gets a bigger monthly check, he receives it for fewer years. He receives only $190,464 total, compared with the $215,040 he would have gotten by retiring at age 62—not to mention the pleasure of extra years of leisure.

Of course, Nick probably isn't framing the keep-working-or-retire decision in terms of his lifetime total in Social Security income. When Nick makes this decision, he'll be asking himself, *How badly do I want to quit working?* versus *Is $1,131 a month going to be enough?* The answer to that is going to depend largely on how much money Nick has saved up. Remember, Social Security is insurance, not a retirement plan in itself. So if Nick does a good job in pulling his finances together and saving at a higher rate—the things I recommended for him in Chapter Two—he'll be more likely to have enough post-retirement income to retire earlier than 70.

However, there's a problem. All of this assumes that Nick can work as late in life as he chooses. That's not necessarily the case. Nick might decide to stay at his job into his late 60s, but the realities of life as a bus driver—the physical stress and the potential medical issues—make it unlikely he'll be able to. He's going to need to find another job if he's going to keep working until the government's normal retirement age, or even to age 70. Nick is faced with the prospect of something he thought he'd left behind years ago: job hunting. Is he going to be welcome in the job market at age 60-something?

Are you?

Nick's age at retirement	Decrease of the benefit received at age 70 if Nick is born in 1960	Amount of monthly check
62	43%	$1,131
63	40%	$1,190
64	36%	$1,270
65	31%	$1,375
66	25%	$1,481
67	20%	$1,587
68	13%	$1,730
69	6%	$1,857
70	0%	$1,984

If Nick works until age 70, he'll receive 100 percent of his benefit, as opposed to a 43 percent decrease if he collects at 62. It's a great opportunity for retirees like Nick, who are behind in their savings later in life. If Nick lives past age 75, he'll have gotten higher benefits than he would have if he'd started collecting at age 62.

When 60 is the new 17

Here's an interesting fact about the current normal retirement age: The Social Security Act of 1935 set that age at 65. Why the change to 67? According to the Social Security website, "Congress cited improvements in the health of older people and increases in average life expectancy as primary reasons for increasing the normal retirement age." Currently, there are calls for the retirement age to be raised to age 70, again citing gains in average longevity. According to supporters of this idea, people can easily work longer because they are living longer.

Things just aren't that simple. Yes, on average, life expectancies in America are rising. But averages aren't everyone. Almost all the gains in longevity have gone to higher-than-average-income earners. In addition, those educated, affluent people are the ones most likely to be welcome in the workplace late in life, as part-time consultants or emeritus professors. Of course, highly educated people also are the least likely to need work at that age, since they usually had the means to save enough for retirement.

For people who spent their lives farther down the income scale, the prospects aren't nearly as shiny. Former line cooks don't usually set up successful consulting firms on line-cooking issues, and I don't think I've ever seen a 70-year-old "bricklayer emeritus" spreading mortar two mornings a week just to keep himself busy. Many elders are forced to take poor-quality jobs in retail and service; most employers won't train older workers, and in soft labor markets, age discrimination is rampant. In short, it's a catch-22: Those most likely to need work late in life are the least likely to find it.

The new face(s) of retirement planning

G ender is a largely unspoken issue in retirement planning. Knock on the door of an 80-year-old and there's a 70 percent chance a woman will answer and that she lives alone. For more about this topic, look at Susan Jacoby's book *Never Say Die: The Myth and Marketing of the New Old Age*. It includes a chilling essay about a lonely old woman on a bus; it's a sharp, sobering look at the realities of senior citizen–hood in twenty-first-century America.

Since the 1970s, the number of single women in the United States has grown dramatically. With the stigma attached to divorce and single motherhood waning, women took advantage of the increasing number of jobs and opportunities available to them. However, they also found their access to economic resources— from equal pay to pensions—severely limited in an economy built around the assumed norm of a nuclear family and male full employment. In response, women organized. They formed groups like the Older Women's League and the Alliance for Displaced Homemakers.

Today, gay men and gay women face challenges in a system made for heterosexual couples and widows. So far, most of the retirement-advice books assume a dad and mom in their golden years, or a widowed mom. But the world doesn't fit so conveniently into that framework anymore.

If you're over 62, lower your wage expectations, and use the income to delay collecting Social Security, if you can.

But let's say you want and need to work after age 65. Your first choice, most likely, would be to simply stay at the job you have now. If only that were always possible! Maybe your company wants to replace you with a young recent graduate they can hire at a starting salary. Or they're cutting back to a smaller workforce overall. Or they're moving jobs overseas. For you, the result is the same: unemployment.

If you can't stay with your longtime employer, probably your second choice is to stay in the same field. But as you search for open positions in that field, you're competing once again with those young recent graduates. It's the classic matchup: Age and Experience versus Youth and Energy. Older workers have solid résumés and years of practical know-how, but young job applicants are willing to work for lower pay to get experience. They have few medical problems that'll interfere with productivity, and health insurance costs less for young people. Many can pull all-nighters because they have no children to care for. Finally, they're usually up to speed on the newest forms of technology. It's easy to see why they're so attractive to the human-resources department.

If you can't stay in your current job, or even your current field, where do you look for work? Your last resort is likely to be a low-skilled position in retail or the service sector. (Put another way: "Well, I can always be a Walmart greeter!") These jobs almost never pay as much as the one you left. Seventy isn't really the new 50. Increasingly, it's the new 17. (And I'm talking about income here, not sex.)

This may not hurt just your pride; it will hurt your bottom line as well. According to the Government Accountability Office, when laid-off older workers do get rehired—and not all do—they take an average 15 percent hit in wages.

Another piece of grim news—I know they've been coming thick and fast—is this: Employers may not be thrilled to see you coming when you're applying for those retail or service jobs. *New York Times* reporters Steve Greenhouse and Michael Barbaro reported on an embarrassing internal memo to Walmart's board of directors in 2005 that discussed ways to discourage older workers from seeking or staying at jobs at Walmart stores. Among the methods, which were characterized as "ways to hold down spending on health care and other benefits," were ensuring that every job required physical tasks—stocking shelves, gathering carts—that older and less healthy workers would find difficult. Even when you're not applying to work at a big-box store, the labor market can be tough all around. A friend of mine, laid off at 53, was sent to job counseling for executives. In part, the counselor's blunt advice was "Lose weight and take Prozac."

Bear in mind, layoffs aren't the only thing standing between you and working past age 65. Poor health is the enemy of productivity. Illness and disability rob many people first of their jobs and then of their appeal to potential new employers. And don't forget, it's not just you who might get sick. The health problems of a spouse or partner can take nearly as heavy a toll. According to a McKinsey & Company survey, 40 percent of workers are forced to retire earlier than they had planned, with their health or the health of a family member the reason cited for more than half of those early retirements.

A FEW WAYS TO BEAT THE ODDS

Ultimately, no matter how much you want to work later in life, a job may not be there for you. That's partly what this chapter is about: helping you face the difficult truth that the workplace might let go of you before you're ready to leave. In light of that, the other aspects of your retirement plan—how you save, invest, and even vote—become even more important.

But because many older people want and need to keep working, here are some ways to increase your appeal to employers.

One, stay technologically literate. "Hey, don't look at me," you might be saying. "It's not like I'm still on MySpace." But technological proficiency isn't a destination, it's a journey. An ongoing one. You might feel you're up to speed now, but someday you'll tell a younger coworker that you're going to text them, and they'll say, "What is this, 2016? Don't text me, just brainwave me on my neurotenna!" It'll happen before you know it.

Don't spike the ball on the 40-yard line. Keep moving forward. There are advantages to tech literacy that go beyond how hirable you look to an employer. First, advances in technology tend to make jobs easier, not harder—if they didn't, they wouldn't replace old methods. Second, jobs that require technological proficiency tend to be desk jobs, which will be the kind you'll need if you have age-related physical limitations.

Two, get midcareer education. You wouldn't want an operation to be done by a surgeon who finished his residency in 1998 and then never updated his skills; you'd want somebody who's kept on top of new procedures and techniques. What applies to medicine applies to many other fields. It isn't just elite professionals who need midcareer education. Software and technological devices are used in a great many fields, and they're constantly changing. And that's not all. New machines, new markets, new techniques, new ideas, new priorities . . . You'll face some or all of those over the course of a long career. Be interested, be engaged, and embrace change.

Three, make and keep friends in your line of work. Yes, *networking* was one of the most ubiquitous buzzwords of the 1990s. But networking was a popular concept for a reason: It paid off. It still does. If you've been laid off, connections and goodwill are incredibly important to getting that next job. People will pick up the phone and talk to someone they know and like. They're much less likely to answer a phone message with an unfamiliar name and number attached.

Four, scale back your expectations. As we've already noted, it'd be ideal to keep working in your chosen field, the one in which you've spent most of your career. But that may not be possible. Statistics tell us that employers in manufacturing, finance, insurance, wholesale trade, scientific and technical services, arts and entertainment, and the recreation industry all have a strong bias toward hiring younger people. However, older workers may find jobs in home health care (quite the irony: old people taking care of old people), retail trade, management, administrative support, waste management services, education, health care, and the social assistance sector.

The point: The job that's open may not be the job you want. You might be thinking, *I'll pack it in and retire before I work behind a bakery counter.* That's your prerogative. But always remember the 30 percent reduction in your Social Security check that you face if you retire at age 62 on the one hand, and on the other, the premium you'll get by staying employed until 70. The government is giving you an incentive to stay in the workforce; it's in your best interest to take it. For that reason, you'll need to be both determined and humble when job hunting.

———————

So far, I've asked you to look at some hard truths and to do some painful calculations. I've asked you to estimate your own life span. Then I asked you to calculate how much money you'll need for retirement and to take a clear-eyed look at how far off track you are in getting there. Finally, I've pointed out that you might not be able to work late in life, no matter how much you want to. (It's not for nothing that economics is called the dismal science.)

But now we're going to look at solutions. In the next chapter I discuss the role savings will play in getting you back on track to retire, and some practical ways you can trim your spending.

Chapter Four:

Saving, Spending, and Debt.

Or, how to keep your head above water in "the richest nation in the world!"

merica is a funny place. For one thing, ask the average person on the street, and they'll likely tell you the United States is the richest nation on the planet.

Actually, as measured by the commonly used yardstick of gross national product per person, the United States tends to hover around sixth- to seventh-richest from year to year. Norway, Singapore, and Switzerland are all richer than we are (with the remaining nations being oil sheikdoms or secret tax havens).

Why do so many Americans have this misconception about the United States? In part, it's because of the sheer size and spending power of our middle class. Compared with nations in which wealth is concentrated in the hands of the few, in America, middle-class families often vacation abroad, and even working-class families own houses and cars. This isn't the state of affairs in most of the world. To the rest of the planet, America looks like one big wonderland of prosperity.

So why do so many of us feel poor? Why do we lie awake worrying about money?

One reason is Americans' famous tendency to consume. From the moment we wake up in the morning until we go to bed at

Overspending: a wider perspective

A dvice on how to trim your budget and slash spending is everywhere. Newspaper features, magazine articles—even entire books are devoted to the subject. Seeing all of them, you could easily conclude that if you don't have savings, it's all your fault.

But just as our car-dependent society and the availability of cheap sugary and fatty foods contribute to the obesity crisis, so the financial environment contributes to the retirement-security crisis. It isn't the faulty American character that causes us to have less in retirement savings than we need. Americans pay more for medical care, child care, education, costs of unemployment, disability, and nursing home and at-home care for older folks than most people in the 36-member club of rich nations, the Organization for Economic Cooperation and Development (OECD). And Americans have less affordable and reliable public transportation than most OECD nations.

Although cutting spending is obviously a subject of great interest to us in America, and I'm not going to discourage you from trimming your budget, most likely hyper-consumerism is not the cause of inadequate retirement savings. The lack of basic public services, social insurance, and inadequate retirement vehicles is. That's why voting to protect Social Security and Medicare, and to expand safe pensions at election time, is part of a good retirement plan.

night, we're part of a huge machine designed to separate us from our money. Asking people to save money in America is like asking them to give up chocolate. Spending—and its partner, credit—is deeply ingrained in American life. "You deserve it!," we're constantly told by advertisements and the media, plus, "You get what you pay for" and, "It's an investment" (even if whatever *it* is will have virtually no resale value at all once we walk out of the store with it).

If your money is slipping out of your hands, and you can't figure out where it all went . . . well, you probably had some help spending it as quickly as you did.

But it's actually possible to visit Hershey, Pennsylvania, and not eat chocolate. And it's possible to live in America and not overspend. I've listened to quite a few people talk about how they intend to bridge the gap between the money they have and what they'll need for retirement. Sometimes the ideas are good ones. Sometimes, frankly, they're not. Here are some ideas I'd rather you ruled out.

Bad Idea #1: "I can always live with my kids." Yes, the romantics say that the multigenerational family is going to have to be re-created to solve the retirement crunch. Admittedly, there's charm to this idea, but financially, it's not a magic bullet. Why? Because in America, the greatest predictor of a person's wealth is the economic status of his or her parents. According to a 2012 Pew Charitable Trusts report, more than 40 percent of people who grew up in the bottom 20 percent of the income scale were still there in adulthood. The rest didn't make it too much higher on the ladder: Fewer than a third had ascended to middle-class status or better. Working-class and lower-middle-class parents usually raise working-class and lower-middle-class kids.

The result: The more likely you are to need to live with your adult children, the less likely they are to have the space or resources to help you out. This is the same catch-22 we saw with working past age 65: It's a strategy most available to the people who need it least. Also, it's rarely the best solution in terms of everyone's mental health: Adult kids often don't want to live with their parents, and older people value their independence.

Bad Idea #2: "I'll move to a state with lower taxes!" Sure, it's a plan. But it's a screwy plan. Yes, film directors shoot movies in states that offer tax advantages. But you're not going to be there for a 12-week shooting schedule; this is your life. Are you going to want to leave friends, family, traditions, a favorite restaurant, and the familiar view from your front window—all for a marginal difference in tax rates? Even big businesses factor in these kinds of personal preferences when deciding where to make their headquarters. One study found that an influential factor in where businesses are headquartered is whether the CEO wants to live there. The tax advantage is a secondary consideration.

Bad Idea #3: "I'll read investment newsletters and magazines!" Seems counterintuitive, right? How can increasing your financial know-how be a bad thing? Yet statistics tell us it is. Study after study shows that people confident in their investment skills tend to trade frequently; they also trade on current news. The problem is that frequent trading increases your brokerage fees, cutting into your profits. And trading on the day's headlines is just as bad. Current news to the world at large is news that's been expected and taken into consideration by the pros, who have already sold and moved on. But the self-taught, investment-magazine-reading investor is preparing to buy high in hopes a stock

> Paying off a loan is always your best investment. No matter what the interest rate is, when you pay it off you get a guaranteed return, equal to the interest rate. Paying off a credit card with a 15 percent interest earns you a guarantee of, well, 15 percent.

will go higher, and he or she is likely to sell low-earning assets to pay for it. In short, they're buying high and selling low. You don't need to be an economist to understand why that's a bad idea.

People who read about investing a lot are confident. In most areas of life, that's a good thing. It certainly is when you're walking into the boss's office to negotiate a raise, or approaching an attractive stranger at a cocktail party. But in the stock market, false confidence is your enemy.

Now that we've covered some of the bad ideas, here are a few good ones.

Good Idea #1: Downsize now; live on 70 percent of your income. As I've discussed, very few people will have retirement income that equals what they were making during their working lives. Seventy percent is approximately the highest rate most people can hope for.

It's true that some expenses will go away after retirement: As I noted before, you won't have a commute anymore, for example, and you'll no longer be setting aside savings. (Remember that, ideally, savings should be a monthly budget item like everything else during your whole working life.) But new costs will arise. You'll be going to the doctor more, and Medicare and health insurance won't pay 100 percent of your expenses. You might also, if you have health or mobility problems, pay other people to cut your grass or clean your home.

The upshot is that to avoid a jarring drop in your standard of living in old age, you'll need to learn to live well on that 70 percent now. It's easier and mentally healthier to make new choices and develop better habits while you're still in your 30s and forming spending norms with your partner, children, and peers. Being forced into a Spartan way of life in your 60s or 70s is very depressing.

Plus, there's an obvious corollary: When you trim your spending, it'll free up money to pay down debt and contribute to savings.

Good Idea #2: Have a nice home in a modest neighborhood. Humans have lived in clans and villages forever, so we've been influenced by each other forever . . . sometimes to our detriment. Although the media and popular culture encourage you to buy as expensive a home as you can afford, that may be bad for your finances in ways that go beyond the monthly mortgage. Living in a high-income neighborhood is likely to nudge you into a more lavish lifestyle in emulation of how the people around you are spending their money: Being around affluent people makes affluence seem normal. What's above average for the nation becomes average to you if you see it every time you step out the front door.

Consider bucking the trend and living in a more affordable part of town. Not only will your mortgage or rent and household expenses be lower, but you'll have a pleasant sense of your own prosperity and, perhaps, a greater appreciation of what you have.

Compounding:
Don't let it work against you

Compounding can be your best friend or your worst enemy—and it's the latter when you're carrying a balance on a credit card. Thanks to compounding, you don't pay interest only on your principal, you pay interest on the interest—and the total amount can really snowball over time. I talk about how compounding can work for you in Chapter Five. For now, let's talk about its power to undermine wealth, using an example I put together with the help of dinkytown.net (the site with the cool, free calculators).

Say you owe $7,000 on a credit card. You're paying 18 percent interest and making the minimum monthly payment of $280. If you continue to pay the minimum, it will take you 11 years and 8 months to pay off this debt, and the total interest you'll have paid will be $4,071. But if you decide to pay $25 extra per month—a "roll-down" strategy—you will pay off your card in 2 years and 5 months, and will pay only $1,641 in interest—$2,430 less.

Yet more good ideas. There's no single magic bullet; saving is a combination of many small efforts. The following ten propositions are based on sound economic research.

1. Keep a budget and record everything that you buy. The first step in getting control of your spending is just being aware of it. This simple act of focusing your attention on where your money is going tends to reduce spending by 15 percent.

Of course, this strategy will quickly be undermined if you add to the balance on your card by making new purchases. So once you've started, keep your hands off that card. And when you've paid off the card, get in the habit of paying your balance monthly, because the typical 15 percent interest rate is just too high. Consider this: Before the 1970s, extending loans at rates higher than 10 percent typically violated state usury laws (and credit cards are essentially loan vehicles). It was considered "loan sharking," or charging excessively high rates to people who couldn't get loans anywhere else and were desperate. This practice was mostly the province of organized-crime syndicates. But in the 1970s, usury laws were eliminated. Banks got in the business of issuing credit cards and extending other loans to people with low incomes.

Banks also used to set minimum repayments at levels so low, the balance was never paid off, and the debtor kept paying interest on interest. Fortunately, consumer protection laws over the years have slowly made credit-card companies set minimum payments at a level that will allow a debtor to eventually pay off the loan.

2. Don't carry an ongoing balance on your credit card. Too many people use credit cards as quick cash for everyday purchases, and about 50 percent of them carry a balance from month to month, incurring interest charges. It's better to carry a debit card with a credit-card function. It will carry a balance, but only for a month, at which point you have to pay it off. Your actual credit card should stay at home in a hard-to-reach place. It'll be there in case of a true emergency.

3. Watch less television. What? Isn't television low-cost entertainment, and isn't anything low cost good for a frugal lifestyle? The point here is that TV has an insidious hidden
cost: the cost of things you'll probably buy if you're a frequent viewer. The reason for this extra spending is twofold.
First, TV watchers are exposed to commercials, which we
like to think we're ignoring but that are crafted by experts
to linger in our minds and urge us to buy. Second, rich char-
acters are overrepresented on television shows, and even the
working-class ones have great apartments, expensive haircuts, and stylish clothes. It skews our ideas of what's realistic and attainable. Watching less television is like turning
down the volume on an endless appeal to spend.

4. Rethink life insurance. If you don't have kids, you almost certainly don't need it. But if you do have life insurance, make
sure it's term, not whole. Term life insurance is insurance
pure and simple: You pay premiums and get a lump sum if
the insured dies. Whole life insurance has an increasing value
that the insured can cash out or borrow from; it's an insurance policy that also acts as an investment. Unfortunately,
it's not a good investment, because the product is inflexible
and the fees are high. If you've ever tried that peanut butter and jelly that comes in the same jar, and didn't care for
it—well, this is pretty much the same. Insurance and investments work better when they're two separate things.

5. Speaking of insurance, raise the deductible on every policy you have; that will reduce your monthly premiums. The
deductible is the amount of money you have to pay on a loss
before your insurance company steps in and pays the rest.
If you agree to pay a higher share, you get a lower monthly
premium. For example, if you raise your home-insurance

deductible from $500 to $1,000, you can save almost 25 percent on your premium. This works similarly for auto and health insurance. Bottom line: Insurance is there so that a huge misfortune won't wipe you out financially; that's clearly worthwhile. But don't pay high premiums month after month to avoid any unexpected expense.

6. Similarly, never buy a protection policy for an appliance; many are quite reliable and run for years without problems. If one does break, take it back to the store; it's almost certainly covered by a warranty you got for free, usually a year (enough time to know if the product is faulty).

7. As soon as you've bought a car, start saving for the next one. Then, when the time comes, buy a car you can pay for with cash. Notice that I say "a car," not "a new car." According to the Department of Transportation, in 2007 there were 254.4 million passenger vehicles in the United States—this for a population of about 300 million people, not all of whom drive. There's absolutely no reason to buy brand-new with so many high-quality used cars out there. Need a better reason? According to Bankrate.com, most new cars lose 20 percent of their value as soon as you drive them off the lot and another 20 percent off that in the first year. Likewise, don't waste money on the extras, including an extended warranty. *Consumer Reports* found that most owners spent more on extended warranty insurance than they would have on repairs. Cars today are manufactured with better steel, meaning rustproofing and undercoating aren't worth the cost.

8. Eating out? Try a trick restaurant owners say diners use during big economic recessions. People go out, but they often forgo beverages and dessert. Eat out and trim the bill. Enjoy the bread, though—it's free, and probably contains fewer

calories than the drink and dessert you were going to buy, saving about 20 percent on your bill. (It's weird, I know, but sometimes I put butter and sugar on a piece of bread and call it dessert, like my recession-traumatized Italian grandmother used to do.)

9. Speaking of dinner, eat your vegetables. Get a little exercise, too. Doesn't sound like financial advice, you say? It is. Health problems can profoundly undermine your savings, because insurance doesn't cover everything.

10. I've saved the best for last: Don't carry a mortgage any longer than you have to. A 7- or 15-year option, rather than the high-priced 30-year standard, will certainly raise your monthly payment, but you'll save money in the long run—partly because of a lower interest rate, but largely because you've halved the time the loan is racking up interest. This is a good option for people who use a mortgage and house as a kind of mandatory savings plan. If you put most of your discretionary income toward your mortgage, you are storing your wealth in something you also consume. In other words, while you're paying the bank, you're also accruing savings. So, paying off the mortgage as early as possible is one of the best deals around. You instantly get a rate of return equal to the interest rate you pay to the bank. This topic is so significant, I'm going to talk about it at length.

Paying off debt: even better than saving?

A true story: A brilliant scientist who had just won a major prize—not the Nobel, but one that awarded him more than

$300,000—asked me if he should invest in euro-weighted derivatives. (Don't worry if you don't know what that means; in fact, it's part of the point I'm making—that he was considering such an obscure investment.) In response, I asked him a simple question: "Do you have a mortgage?"

> First and foremost, put any extra money toward paying off your mortgage.

"Yes," he said.

"Pay it off instead," I told him. "That's a sure thing; the derivatives are not."

He was stunned. Let's think about that a minute: Here was a man who understood the workings of the universe, but he didn't understand why it was better to get out of debt than to put his money into an esoteric investment with no guaranteed rate of return—in fact, an investment so iffy, he risked losing every cent.

Let's explore some interest-rate math. Let's say you have 15 years left on your mortgage with $100,000 outstanding. Your mortgage rate is a low 5 percent, and as a median earner, your tax bracket is 30 percent (combined state and federal). That means that you can deduct 30 percent of the interest you pay, if you itemize on your taxes. (I say *if* for a reason; we'll get to that shortly.)

Now let's say that you have $100,000 on your hands. (Where'd it come from? Maybe you pushed Bill Gates out of the way of a speeding bus, and in gratitude, he took out his wallet and gave you $100,000 on the spot. Just go with it; I'm making a point.) You consider paying off your mortgage, but then decide that you'll hang on to it, reasoning that you need the tax deduction that you get from your mortgage interest and that you'll find a better investment for your $100,000.

But that reasoning is invalid. Here's why. Over the 15 years that it will take you to pay off your mortgage, you'll pay a little more than $42,000 in interest to the bank. Ick. But you justify it because of that 30 percent tax break. It's true that you will save about $12,700 on your tax bill over those 15 years—but that's out of $42,000 total, leaving about $29,000 in total interest paid. However, if you use your $100,000 to pay off your mortgage? You're immediately $29,000 ahead. That's a non-taxable 29 percent return on investment!

But wait, it gets better. This is where I'll explain the *if* part of *if you itemize*. The truth is, unless you're a high earner with other things to itemize on your 1040, you're usually better off taking the standard deduction. At the time of this book's writing, the standard deduction was $6,100 for single people and married filing separately, and higher for heads of household and marrieds filing jointly. For example, consider a single, middle-income person who's in the first year of a 30-year, $100,000 mortgage with a 5 percent interest rate. If he has only that mortgage interest to itemize, he'd be far better off taking the $6,100 standard deduction (which would lower his taxes by $1,708) than taking the $5,000 deduction for mortgage interest (which would lower his taxes by only $1,400). In other words, it is generally true that unless the amount you pay in interest on your mortgage in a year exceeds the standard deduction for that year, you're better off taking the standard deduction. And in that circumstance, you actually aren't saving anything on your taxes by paying mortgage interest! (For the sake of clarity, I'm leaving out state taxes here. State tax rates vary, but in general are low enough that my example remains true, even including your state income tax.)

Remember, the tax code is influenced by households in the very top brackets. The tax breaks for home mortgages, IRAs, 401(k) plans, capital gains, and so on are worth a lot more to people in the top 2 percent of earners (people making about $250,000 or more). But the standard deduction and earned income tax credit helps households from the upper middle class on down.

Let's go back to you, with your hypothetical $100,000 outstanding on the mortgage and your hypothetical $100,000 from Bill Gates. Assuming that you're not in the top 2 percent of earners (that elite $250,000-plus club), you're better off taking the standard deduction, rendering the mortgage-interest tax break completely irrelevant. Therefore, over 15 years you'd pay nearly $43,000 in interest on your mortgage. Which means that if you use your $100,000 to pay off the mortgage now, you won't save only the $29,000 that a higher-earning taxpayer would save after using the mortgage deduction, you'll save the entire $43,000. Over 15 years, this averages out to the equivalent of an investment with a 2.8 percent annual return, *risk-free*. Those last two words are italicized for a reason: It's the most important point here. There's absolutely no chance that your investment will tank or even underperform. There's no market fluctuation or adverse news events that can undercut it. It's guaranteed. And that's a great deal.

The only argument for carrying a mortgage that makes sense to me—and only barely—is that it "automates" savings for people who wouldn't save otherwise. Having a mortgage requires people to put money into their home every month that they probably would have spent otherwise. So, in essence, some people pay the bank to keep them from spending—I admit I did it once. But it's an expensive service. You'll be better off if you pay off your mortgage and start investing the money you save going forward. Whether you pay off your mortgage in one lump sum or by paying extra over time, you're helping yourself to an easier retirement.

This is true for any kind of loan—not just a mortgage. The

same logic holds for a car loan or for credit-card debt. It doesn't make sense to set money aside in savings while you have month-to-month debt. This is especially true if you're putting those savings into a very low-risk vehicle like a passbook savings account. Why earn 0.1 percent interest on your savings (looks like a misprint, doesn't it?) while paying 15 to 18 percent interest on your credit card or 2 to 6 percent on a car loan?

Bottom line: There are two sides to the interest rate. Either you're earning interest, or you're paying it. As often as possible, be on the earning side. Remember that Number 7 on my list of ways to save money was that you start saving for your next car as soon as you've bought one? To take this idea a little further, consider a "car savings account." If you're making payments on your car, as soon as it's paid off, immediately start putting the same amount into a savings account toward the next car. The goal is to never have a car loan again.

Yes, it'll be painful to give up on the idea of taking that money and putting it toward other expenses (or indulgences). But since you've been making that payment for several years, it's impossible to argue that you can't afford to set it aside now. More important, it's an easy jump from the paying to the earning side of the interest equation.

_____

Now, let's say you've followed the steps above. Congratulations, you're a clear-sighted, responsible saver! But you can't just stick the money in a coffee can—or, just as bad, a bank savings or checking account. You need to invest it.

But should you do that yourself? Do you need a financial adviser, and if so, how do you find the right one? This is a tricky area, and it's what I'm going to discuss next.

Chapter Five:
Investing and Allocation.
Or, "I have this Guy . . ."

f Jane Austen were alive today, she'd probably say that it is a truth universally acknowledged that a man or woman in possession of a fortune must be in want of a financial manager. In fact, you don't even need a fortune: If you're remotely middle class in America, almost inevitably you'll get hooked up with an investment adviser. Or, as I like to say, a "Guy."

Your Guy doesn't have to be a guy; some are women. The result, though, is the same. "Jeff called. He wants me to sell some bonds and buy FROOFROO stock. He suggested ten thousand dollars' worth, but I said only five thousand." Or, "My Guy is pretty good. He always calls, and he doesn't push me into investments."

Sounds okay so far, right? But when I ask people how much the Guy costs, they don't really know. When I ask if he has fiduciary loyalty, they don't know what that means. When I ask if the investments he puts them in do better than a standard benchmark like the S&P 500 index, again, they don't know.

The Guy rarely takes into account anyone's taxes or debt levels, or other real issues about their lives. The Guy lives on commissions. In fact, many Guys are essentially in sales, with a working knowledge of financial terms. Many couldn't pass a basic financial literacy test.

A definition of terms here: *Fiduciary loyalty* essentially means an ethical obligation to you, the customer. Helaine Olen, author of *Pound Foolish: Exposing the Dark Side of the Personal Finance Industry,* explains it this way: If you bought a pair of shoes from a store that had fiduciary loyalty, it would be the store's responsibility to make sure those shoes really fit you before you left. Similarly, a fiduciary money manager can be sued if he or she doesn't give you financial advice that's solely in your interest.

The news about money managers isn't all bad. There are fee-only certified financial planners who are independent and free of conflicts of interest. They don't sell investment products, and they don't work on commission. Such a professional will charge you up front to create a financial plan, similar to the way a lawyer would charge to draw up a will. This service might cost you $1,000 or more, but you'll save money in the long run.

One caveat here: Fee-only advisers tend to be pretty rare outside cities, so you may have difficulty finding one if you live in a smaller town. However, the good news is that you may not even need a manager. To understand why, you have to understand what passive management and active management are.

A passively managed fund is one in which the manager takes a hands-off approach, usually by following a stock or bond index. One such stock index is the Russell 3000, which contains the stocks of approximately 98 percent of the investable U.S. market. (In other words, when you invest in a fund that follows the Russell 3000, you are investing in 98 percent of U.S. companies at one time.) Smaller, but better known, is the S&P 500. Introduced by Standard & Poor's in 1957, it follows the 500 largest publicly traded companies. This index is widely used to measure the general level of stock prices (though the Dow—which contains 30 high-profile stocks—steals all the headlines).

A fund that tracks the S&P 500, therefore, will mirror the general performance of the stock market overall. You won't be protected from the usual fluctuations. It will go up and down. But over time, the market has always gained ground.

In contrast, an actively managed fund is one whose manager chooses stocks in an effort to outperform the market. Some managers do succeed at this—for a time. But the statistics show that such hot streaks always end. Studies done on actively managed mutual funds have been clear on this point: Past performance is a very unreliable predictor of future returns.

Professor Jeremy Siegel explains this in detail in his book *Stocks for the Long Run*. Using mutual-fund data provided by the Vanguard Group and Lipper Analytical Services, he found that all actively managed equity mutual funds returned an average of 10.49 percent per year for the period 1971 to 2006, whereas the S&P 500 rose an average of 11.53 percent.

It's worth noting two things here (as Siegel did). First, the funds benefited from a stellar run for small stocks between 1975 and 1983 (this likely helped actively managed funds—managers find smaller stocks attractive because of their growth potential). Over the period of 1984 to 2006, after the run was finished, actively managed funds returned an average of only 10.8 percent yearly compared with the S&P 500's 12.26 percent. Second, and more important, the actively managed fund figures don't reflect the impact of sales and redemption fees.

And now we've arrived at a crucial point: It isn't whether your fund manager can beat the market and for how long; what really chips away at your savings when you invest in an actively managed fund is how much your manager charges. Passive management can be done very cheaply, by virtue of its hands-off approach. Index funds tend to charge about 0.1 percent of the

Six critical questions to ask your Guy

1. How are you paid? Fee-only advisers receive no compensation from the sale of investment products. All others do. You can't count on an adviser who gets a significant portion of their pay in sales commissions. Period. Leave if they are not fee-only.

2. Do you have any conflicts of interest that influence the advice you provide? Financial advisers who are registered representatives get paid to sell insurance or annuity products promoted by their brokers. Ask how they choose the investments they recommend. Ask them directly how they are paid.

3. Will my assets be housed with an independent custodian—that is, a bank that is not selling the investment products? "Yes" is the only acceptable answer here. Bernie Madoff's firm did not use an independent custodian. Enough said.

4. Are your clients similar to me? If your adviser's typical client is worth $1 million or more, and you aren't rich, think twice. Your adviser may lean toward advice more suited to his or her richest clients.

5. What services do you provide? If the adviser's primary service is investment advice, and you want a complete financial plan, this adviser is unlikely to be a good match.

6. Do you act in a fiduciary capacity toward your clients? Leave fast if the adviser doesn't say yes. You are asking the broker if he or she is obligated to put your interest first, before that of his or her firm. If there is any other answer but a clear yes, grab your wallet tight and leave.

total investment in fees; they pass the savings on to you. Active management, by nature, costs more. These expenses, likewise, are passed along. Usually, the cost is about 2 percent.

To illustrate this, let's revisit that $100,000 you got from Bill Gates in Chapter Four. This time, let's say you don't have a mortgage to pay off, so you're free to invest in a mutual fund. Now you have a choice: an index fund or one with a fund manager who chooses stocks in an attempt to beat the market. Once you pick a fund, you stay in it for, let's say, ten years.

During those ten years, the S&P 500 rises by 5 percent a year, and both funds match that in performance. Naturally, the index fund does, because it tracks the S&P. The other fund does it through skilled stock-picking by its manager. (This is statistically unlikely, especially over a ten-year period. In fact, it's almost certain that an actively managed fund would return less than the S&P 500. But we'll assume it for the sake of argument.) So after ten years, that $100,000 has grown into $163,000, through the power of compounding.

Let's pause here and talk about compounding again, because it's that important. Remember the runaway growth of your credit-card balance in the example I provided earlier, the one in which you made only the minimum payment? Interest compounding in savings works the same way (only now it's not quite so "runaway," since market returns, averaged over time, aren't as high as credit-card interest rates). But the key point is the same: You earn interest on your principal and interest on your returns, meaning the picture just gets better over time. The earlier you start and the longer you can keep your money invested (meaning no early withdrawals), the more the miracle of compounding works for you.

So in our example, if you invest $100,000 at 5 percent per year, in ten years that money will have turned into $163,000.

Except that won't be the balance on the statement you get in year ten, whether you invested in an actively managed or a passively managed account. It'll be less than $163,000. Why? Because of fees.

If you go with an index fund, you'd end up with $161,000. That's because index funds charge one-tenth of 1 percent of the assets under management, so instead of earning 5 percent, you're getting 4.9 percent. Because of the math of compounding interest, a 0.1 percent drop in the rate of return leads to a

> **Dump any adviser whose income depends on your decisions. Avoid the "conflicted" adviser and actively managed funds.**

2 percent drop in total return. In your case, that means you paid about $2,000 over the ten years to be in the index fund. Maybe that doesn't thrill you, but remember, an index fund's 0.1 percent fee is about the best you can do, short of writing to every single publicly traded company and enclosing a check for individual stock certificates that are then mailed to your house and that you then store in a gigantic filing cabinet . . . Yikes.

But what happens if you chose an actively managed fund? That's where the math of compounding interest comes home to roost in a big way. Actively managed accounts generally charge up to 2 percent in fees. We've seen that in an index fund every 0.1 percent in fees results in a 2 percent reduction in total return over ten years. So every 1 percent in fees leads to about a 20 percent drop—actually, a bit more, given that we're dealing with compounding and its snowball effect. With a 2 percent fee structure, you get about 46 percent less in total return from an actively managed account over ten years. In our example, your $100,000 investment has grown in the actively managed fund to the same

$163,000. But the fees charged by your manager over time have eaten up $29,000, so you're left with $134,000. None of the difference is caused by your fund's performance; it's all fees.

So if, in ten years' time, you want to fee-shame yourself about your choice, there's no shortage of ways you can do it.

1. I earned 46 percent less than I would have in an index fund.
2. I got a 3 percent return when I could've gotten 4.9 percent.
3. I earned $34,000 instead of $61,000.
4. I paid $29,000 in fees when I could have paid $2,000.

Clear enough? You should also remember one thing: The above example generously assumes that your fund manager matched the market's performance, getting a 5 percent return. But history tells us that, minus a few lucky streaks, managed funds almost invariably underperform the market. I'm reminding you of that because a mutual-fund manager is going to tell you his fund's fees are worth it because his experts' picks will outperform the market. But the statistics tell a different story. Are there ever managers who beat the market several years in a row? Sure. But research shows high flyers generally last a few years at most.

Given this, why would you choose an actively managed fund? You shouldn't. This is one of the biggest mistakes people make. To be absolutely clear: If you're with a broker or any kind of adviser paid on commissions, you should sever that relationship as soon as possible. Honestly, you would be better off earning the Boy Scouts' personal finance merit badge and then trusting what you learn from it than using a "Guy." Simply put: Low-fee index funds are all you need. Vanguard Funds is a one-stop shop in this area. I have no connection to or interest in Vanguard; they just offer an excellent product. You can buy directly from their website.

You might be asking, "But what if I have a high net worth?" My answer is the same. Multibillion-dollar funds, like the Norwegian sovereign wealth fund, are so big that if they make a move, the world moves with them. They make markets. They need to be buying illiquid assets and private equity, et cetera. You don't.

If you still feel that you want someone to guide you through the investing process, get a fee-only adviser and pay up front for a personal plan. If you're part of a couple, make sure that your partner in life and in finances is comfortable with the adviser you choose. Both parties need to feel secure about a decision this big.

401(k) plans revisited

You know by now that I'm no fan of the 401(k)-and-IRA or DIY-model of retirement planning. The 401(k) plan and the IRA—where most 401(k) savings end up—have been so lucrative for banks and brokers, who have a great deal of influence in Washington, D.C., that they aren't going anywhere very soon. So if your employer offers a 401(k) plan instead of a pension, that's the most important tool you have for retirement planning, and you need to use it as well as possible.

Employer 401(k) plans do offer two very useful advantages: First, many employers match funds. The average rate is about 50 cents on the dollar up to 6 percent of your pay. That's 6 percent of the pay that you contribute, meaning that in total, the company matches 3 percent of your salary. If you earn $70,000 a year, your 6 percent contribution equals $4,200. At 50 cents to the dollar, your employer adds $2,100, raising your total to $6,300.

Second, you aren't taxed on the money you contribute to a 401(k), including the employer match, nor are your earnings taxed as the money grows. You'll pay taxes later, when you draw down your savings, but it builds up tax-free in the meantime.

There's a pitfall in the 401(k) structure, though: vesting. If you plan to change jobs after working for your company only a relatively short period of time, you might forfeit some or all of the employer match.

Vesting is both nifty and sneaky. It allows employers not to pay matching funds to employees who quit within a relatively short time—which makes it an incentive for employees to stay in a job. To be vested in a 401(k) means that you've become entitled, fully or partially, to the employer match, and you can keep it upon leaving the company.

To keep 100 percent of the employer match, you have to be fully vested. Some companies use "cliff vesting," which vests employees all at once after a certain waiting period. Other companies use "graded vesting," in which the percentage you're entitled to builds up a little at a time: say, 20 percent after a short initial period, then in increments of 20 percent per year after that. Policies vary, so check with your HR representative about how your company does it. In any event, a company can't make you wait more than five years to get to full vesting.

The point: Provided you don't change jobs frequently, an employer match will increase your 401(k) contribution by 50 percent (usually up to 6 percent of your pay). That's a 50 percent guaranteed return on your investment, which is seven to ten times more than you're likely to get annually from an index fund. And let me say it again—it's guaranteed. It's a great deal.

"Then why, Teresa," you might ask, "have you been saying 401(k) plans have been bad for the average person?" I still believe this, for several reasons, including that the lion's share of the tax breaks go to the top earners who don't need government help to save for retirement. More relevant to what we're discussing here, though, is this: American workers have, in large numbers, failed to contribute consistently and adequately to these accounts.

That has happened for a variety of reasons. Some people put off saving for retirement in favor of saving toward more immediate goals, such as a young couple planning a home purchase. Other people simply lack financial literacy. Unfortunately, these also tend to be people who aren't earning high wages in the first place. They're very likely to say, "I need all of my take-home. I'll think about retirement when I'm fifty."

Even educated people and careful savers can be unclear on the benefits of 401(k) plans and thus fail to benefit from them. To see in more detail how this might happen, let's look at Joe, a theoretical new hire. Joe goes to work at age 25 for a starting salary of $40,000 at a company that makes widgets. The HR rep tells him about the company's 401(k) plan, and Joe thinks about it but decides he's too young to lock up his money so permanently. Joe's not dumb; he understands how retirement plans work and that there'll be a 10 percent tax penalty if he withdraws any savings early. That worries him. What if he wants to buy a house, or he meets the mate of his dreams and wants to finance a really great honeymoon in Cozumel?

Plus, there's vesting to think about. His company uses graded vesting, so he won't be fully vested for five years, and he'll have to give up some of his employer's matching funds if he leaves before then. And that's a possibility. Joe is young and ambitious; he might trade up if he gets a better offer.

No, there are just too many variables for his taste; he doesn't want to lock up his money in a 401(k). Joe decides to save and to put his money in an index fund (I told you he's not dumb), but he does so outside a retirement fund, in a regular account where he can get at it without a tax penalty. However, this means he has to pay taxes as it earns money. He's only in the 25 percent tax bracket, so it doesn't matter all that much, but he does lose a small tax break.

What happens next? Joe stays at his company for six years before changing jobs. During that time, he faithfully deposits 5 percent of his pay in his taxable index fund. Let's say (for ease for calculation) that amount is always $2,000 per year, because in those six years, Joe doesn't get a raise. (Joe is smart and ambitious, but the widget industry is stagnant; widgets are used only by economists who use them to make metaphors.)

During that time, the market rises 5.1 percent annually, with Joe's index fund and its low fee structure giving him a 5 percent annual return. In six years, Joe's investment of $12,000 has grown to $16,574. Sounds good, right? However, Joe gave up his employer match! Had he used his company's 401(k) plan, he'd have more than $26,000—more than a third of it from his employer. Joe paid a high price to keep his money liquid.

There are two important things we should note about Joe's situation. First, had Joe put his savings into a 401(k) account and amassed that $26,936, he would have wanted to be careful when changing jobs. If Joe simply cashed out, all that money would become ordinary income, taxed at his usual rate. Moreover, there would be a 10 percent penalty for taking a withdrawal before retirement age. (Painful, but still a net improvement over investing outside of the 401(k)!) However, a direct rollover to an IRA or his new employer's 401(k) plan would spare Joe all that pain. A rollover, sometimes called a trustee-to-trustee transfer, is not considered a withdrawal and is not subject to tax. However, you pay more fees and you lose a lot of fiduciary protection, so keep your 401(k) in a 401(k). Do not roll it over into an IRA.

The second point is that one reason Joe didn't want to put his money into a 401(k) is that he wanted it available for a home purchase. However, employers have a lot of discretion about allowing 401(k) withdrawals. The IRS allows a variety of tax-penalty-free withdrawals from both IRAs and 401(k) accounts, including a $10,000 IRA withdrawal for first-time home buyers. There are restrictions, of course; if you take this option, you'll probably want to check in with a tax adviser to make sure you're playing safely by IRS rules. The point here, though, is that Joe worried unnecessarily about the lack of liquidity in his 401(k). Had he done his homework, he would have seen that there are ways around it.

Do I like seeing people make use of these exceptions? No. In my opinion, retirement savings are retirement savings; they should not be available for any other purpose. But life is life. The point is, people shouldn't let liquidity worries keep them from saving inside their 401(k) accounts.

Joe would have attained the tidy, nearly-$27,000 sum in a 401(k) account because of not one but several factors: disciplined yearly contributions (the most important), the employer match, the tax break, and the low fees of an index fund (assuming the 401(k) offers an index fund). They all came together, thanks to the power of compounding. Let's explore compounding a little further, by examining what would have happened if Joe had made different decisions.

First, Joe invests in a high-fee mutual fund. Second, because Joe believes the fund will beat the market, he halves his usual contribution of 5 percent of his salary to 2.5 percent (or $1,000 per year), expecting that the return will be high enough to make up for his smaller contribution.

Unfortunately, but unsurprisingly, the fund yields just 3.77

percent after fees and taxes (this is a bit high, but I want to give Joe the benefit of the doubt). The consequences are dire: After six years, Joe has only $8,002. A third scenario might be that Joe had saved that same 2.5 percent inside his employer's 401(k) plan, getting the employer match and the tax break. In that case, he could have raised that amount to $12,320, even in the same high-fee fund. That's better, obviously, though still shy of the amounts he could have amassed by contributing 5 percent yearly to an index fund.

Say it with me: Joe, save in a tax-free 401(k), get your employer match, and don't pay high fees charged by actively managed funds!

The key lesson here is this: It's easy to look at your annual salary and think of it as the main—perhaps the only—factor in how much you can put away for retirement. But it isn't, and Joe proves it. For six years, he earns the same modest salary, but the amount of money he amasses for retirement is highly variable in our scenarios, from approximately $8,000 to almost $27,000. The range could be wider: What if Joe failed to contribute at all during his first two or three years? On the other hand, what if he'd decided to save 10 percent of his salary, even though his employer stopped matching at 6 percent?

Between his savings rate and his choice of a fund to invest in, Joe has a lot of control over how much his retirement savings grow. So do you. It's true that some decisions are harder than others. Choosing to save 5 percent of your salary instead of 2.5 percent can be tough, as can choosing to lock up your money in a retirement account rather than keeping it accessible. However, picking an index fund instead of an actively managed fund is easy.

Unless, of course, you're faced with this dilemma: Your employer's 401(k) plan doesn't offer index funds. Believe me, if this is the case where you work, you're not alone. Employers should be required by law to offer index funds in both major investment vehicles—stocks and bonds—but fewer than half do. You're not powerless, though: Get together with your coworkers and ask your employer to do a housecleaning on the 401(k) choices by getting rid of the high-fee junk and offering index funds.

About allocation and rebalancing

If you've spent any time at all talking to people about investing, you've probably heard this rule of thumb: "Your allocation in stocks should be 100 minus your age." In other words, if you're 40, then 60 percent of your money should be in the stock market, with the rest in bonds and other investments.

Neat and intuitive, isn't it? Also, potentially quite wrong. There's no one-size-fits-all rule for allocation, and I'm not going to provide you with one, either.

What I can tell you is that your allocation should be between stocks and bonds—both in indexed funds, please. Yes, indexes aren't only for stocks. Bond index funds usually follow the Barclays U.S. Aggregate Bond Index (formerly the Lehman Aggregate Bond Index). It has become the predominant benchmark for American bond investors and a benchmark index for many U.S. funds.

Leave the exotic investments for the gamblers and the adrenaline junkies. Take a 50/50 allocation as your starting point and adjust it according to your age, marital status, estimated life span, and whether there are any factors in your life that may require you to need money sooner than you prefer. It's likely that unless you're quite close to retirement and financially comfortable, you'll want to adjust in favor of stocks, toward a 60/40 or 70/30 balance. Stocks offer a better return over the long term, but bonds are lower risk, making them a less anxiety-inducing investment for people who are going to need their money sooner rather than later. Of course, if you're young and can ride out some fluctuations in the market, it's okay to start out with a 100 percent allocation in stocks. In fact, it's wise: They do tend to give you a better return, provided you're in an index fund that tracks the market overall for a low cost.

Which brings up this point: Your circumstances are going to change over time, which means you'll need to rebalance your portfolio from time to time. That means changing the proportion of risky and relatively safe vehicles. As you get older and retirement approaches, you should be shifting toward safer vehicles; generally, that means more in bonds and less in stocks. However, in many years, the best thing to do will be nothing. Once you've set up a solid portfolio according to my advice—or a fee-only adviser has set one up for you—it'll be good for a number of years.

This is important, so I'm going to reiterate: Your annual portfolio review is about balancing risk and return, not about reacting to market fluctuations. Don't panic in down markets. Don't dump losers and chase winners. Even experienced investors make this mistake, but it is a mistake. And remember, if you're in index funds (as I've advised), you won't have a widely varied array of "winners" and "losers" in the first place. You'll just need to keep calm and wait for the market to rebound. A good fee-only adviser will know this as well, so if he or she doesn't suggest changes to your portfolio, don't make any!

Finally, you'll need to do this only once a year. Honestly, an annual review is plenty. It'll keep you from being tempted to

Savings: how steep a climb?

Here's a very basic and realistic situation: A hypothetical 45-year-old wants to retire at 65, but has only $30,000 in a 401(k) account. How much will she need to save to retire comfortably at 65?

Starting at age 45, with 20 years to put money in her 401(k) account, and earning in the middle- or upper-income range of $40,000 to $110,000 per year, our hypothetical worker will need to contribute 20 percent of her pre-tax income every year until retirement. That's a steep rate, I know. But at that rate she'll certainly get the maximum possible in matching employer contribution to her 401(k). With those added funds and a 5 percent annual return, she can achieve a secure retirement.

Admittedly, our hypothetical 45-year-old is going to need a whole lot of financial discipline in the next 20 years. If you're reading this book and you're younger than that, count yourself lucky. It's been said before, but it bears repeating: The younger you are when you start saving, the easier the task is, because of the power of compounding. But if you're older than 45? Older than 50? The road ahead is harder, but the point remains: The best day to start planning and saving for your retirement is today.

time the market. One of the first things I learned about my field is that economists never use the phrase *timing the market*. We know that it's a fool's dream: part of the essential human need to know what's unknowable and control what's uncontrollable.

I look over my investments every November. There's no profound reason behind my choice of month, except that going over my finances just before the holidays keeps me from going overboard when buying gifts.

Your home: investment or liability?

I've just said that your allocation should be split up between stock and bond funds, but I'm aware that for many Americans, there's another significant investment in the picture: their home. Whether your home should be considered an investment or merely a place to live is a debate that's heated up since the subprime-mortgage disaster of the early 2000s. The causes of that debacle are beyond the scope of this book, but it's worth noting that America's fixation on home ownership predates the housing bubble of the 2000s. Since long before that, the real-estate and lending lobbies have been telling Americans (and Congress) that home ownership is essential to happiness and prosperity, that a mortgage-interest deduction is some kind of gift, and a mortgage is "legitimate" debt. It's now virtually an article of faith that "home ownership is the American dream!"

If you think that 300-million-plus people all dream about the same thing, check your math. (Plus, most historians would tell you that inasmuch as there is an "American dream," it is upward mobility, not home ownership per se.) However, there are circumstances in which buying makes sense. Owner-occupied housing is often of better quality than rentals, for example. And in certain markets, at certain times, housing can appreciate so quickly that it outpaces an owner's mortgage costs. These are situations in which it may make more sense to take out a mortgage than to keep renting. Because although buying with cash is the ideal, it isn't feasible for most people—a good rule of thumb is that your home's price should be about 2.5 times your annual income, and saving up that amount is a daunting prospect.

However, as I pointed out in Chapter Two, aging households tend to shrink, as widowhood, divorce, and children leaving the nest reduce household size. In later years, you might find yourself with what I call "too much house." In that case, it'll probably make sense to liquidate, downsizing to a smaller house or even renting. The pro-home-ownership arguments aren't as valid when you reach the downsizing stage.

Here are a few things to consider when deciding if continuing to own a home is right for you.

The tax advantage: Is it worth it? Americans worship at the altar of the Almighty Mortgage-Interest Deduction, but it works out only for people who itemize, which, as I've already pointed out, most lower- and middle-income people don't do, because for them the standard deduction is worth more. Another way of saying this is that most lower- and middle-income folks pay less income tax if they take the standard deduction than if they itemize their deductions. Even if having mortgage interest does nudge you into the territory where it makes sense to itemize, bear in mind that the mortgage-interest deduction pays off most for the highest-income taxpayer.

Let's compare a middle-class person with a federal tax rate of 28 percent and a high earner with a taxable income in excess of $400,000, whose tax rate is about 39 percent. (These rates fluctuate, depending on what Congress does from year to year.) The

Reverse mortgages:
deal or no deal?

The reverse mortgage has become very popular in the last decade or so. Here's how it works: Provided a homeowner is 62 or older, lives in the home, and isn't carrying a mortgage that exceeds the value of the property, he or she can get a loan against it—as a lump sum, a series of monthly payments, or a line of credit—without repaying it. Instead of the monthly payments that a traditional mortgage requires, the interest accrues, giving the lender an ever-larger stake in the property. The loan comes due when the homeowner dies, or sells the home, or, in some cases, defaults on property taxes.

Several things seem to make this kind of loan attractive. First, it allows homeowners to get at their home equity without selling—the appeal to senior citizens, many of whom have spent decades in their homes, is obvious. Second, because the home is collateral, there are no income requirements for this loan. Third, and probably most appealing, is the "no required repayments" clause (though if the homeowner chooses to make payments on the loan, there is no pre-payment penalty).

I'm not sold on reverse mortgages. Neither are the AARP and consumer-protection agencies. These loans tend to have high up-front fees and interest rates. They can be risky for younger retirees, especially if their home is a large part of their net worth. The problem here is that you might spend down the proceeds of the loan and then be left with very little in assets late in life, when costs such as long-term care still loom ahead. A secondary concern is heirs. If it's important to you to leave a substantial estate behind, this is probably not the right loan for you.

The bottom line: These mortgages vary in their terms from lender to lender, and every borrower's situation is different. When in doubt, talk to a fee-only financial planner or look up the excellent articles on reverse mortgages done by AARP.org or Bankrate.com. If you proceed down this road, counseling will be required before you sign, so listen and ask questions.

Of course, the most financially advantageous way to tap the equity in your home is the most obvious—sell it. But another factor plays into that decision: your emotional attachment to the home, something that's hard to put into financial terms. Still, long story short, you'll pay a price for holding on to a large house as a solitary widow or widower, or as a couple with no children living in the home.

All of this circles back to my advice from Chapter Four: Downsize now. If you're ready to start living on 70 percent of your current income, trading down to a smaller home— renting one, in some cases—can get you a long way toward that goal. Plus, there are two advantages to liquidating your house earlier rather than later. One, you'll be diversified, thus safer, right away. Two, you won't put yourself through the stress of a move later in life, and will have time to build up a fund of good memories in your new home. As a result, you'll avoid being emotionally tethered to a property when you're older and it's harder to move.

> Pay off your mortgage.
> You always want to be
> earning interest, not
> paying interest.

middle-class person would save 28 cents in income tax for each dollar of home mortgage interest, whereas the taxpayer in the highest bracket pays 39 cents less per dollar. But either way, both of them are paying a dollar to the bank to get this deduction.

The bottom line: The math never works in an interest payer's favor, but the person with the highest income gets the most help from the government to buy a house and pay the bank interest.

Are you really diversified? If nearly all your net worth is tied up in your house, you're at risk. Your money would be safer in a broad portfolio of stocks and bonds.

And that's a problem. It's hard to lose your entire investment in a house (although as we saw in the recent downturn, it does happen), but you're not shielded against temporary downturns in home values. Nor is a house a liquid asset you can easily tap into in times of need (say, unexpected medical costs). As long as you need to live in your home, its value is mostly an abstraction. Of course, you can borrow against it, but that entails a whole new set of payments alongside your mortgage—with more interest, of course. Great for a lender, not so good for you.

How does rental housing stack up to real estate in your area? The quality of rental housing is good in some places, not so great in others. It may be worth it to buy instead of rent if you'll get a better home for a comparable monthly expense.

A final note about this: As I mentioned before, it often makes sense to sell your home if divorce, widowhood, or grown-and-flown children have reduced your household size, say, from four people to one. Here's a good rule of thumb for whether you should sell your house: How much of your income is going toward your mortgage? If you can barely make the monthly payment, you have too much house. Liquidate, cash in on the equity you have, and invest that money in an index fund.

To see how housing decisions play out in real life, let's revisit two of our hypothetical people from Chapter Two, Jennifer and Paul (pages 42–43).

Jennifer is the 57-year-old real-estate broker earning $125,000 a year. She has $500,000, from a divorce settlement and an inheritance, and she rents her apartment. The money is not in a 401(k) or IRA account. I commented that given Jennifer's goal to work through age 67, as well as her comfortable savings, she was on track for retirement on her terms. However, one dilemma that might arise for her is whether she wants to keep renting for the rest of her life or buy a home. (Given that she's in real estate, we can imagine that Jennifer hears this question from her colleagues a lot.)

My advice is that if Jennifer knows where she wants to settle down permanently, it's a good idea for her to buy a home, especially since as a broker, she's likely to be a very competent negotiator. But she shouldn't be confused by budget experts who advise not spending more than one-quarter to one-third of her monthly income on housing. And neither should you. Here I have figured that Jennifer shouldn't pay more than $180,000 for a house, which will cost her about $10,000 a year in maintenance and taxes. That $10,000 is about 10 percent of her *take home pay*, not one-third to one-quarter of her income. People with lower incomes spend a third of their income on housing; people who have more money and more costly things in their

lives, like travel and expensive health care, spend a smaller portion of their incomes on housing. Also, that expert budget advice
is not for young people who can expect higher incomes as they
grow older. Jennifer is no spring chicken. Earnings fall for workers after age 50, especially for college-educated workers (promotions are less frequent and new jobs often pay less than previous
jobs). Jennifer's basic expenses should be on the conservative
side, so as she ages she has room to pay for expected and unexpected costs of growing older. The bottom line: She should not
buy a more expensive house that will eat up her capital, especially in taxes and maintenance.

If Jennifer were trying to qualify for a 30-year home mortgage, the bank would say that based on her income of $125,000
per year and average interest rates and taxes, she could buy a
home costing as much as $270,000. However, let's say she doesn't
listen to me (or the bank) and buys a $212,000 home, making a
20 percent down payment ($42,400), and taking out a loan of
$169,600 with a 5 percent interest rate. Jennifer would pay more
than $150,000 in interest on that home over 30 years! Granted,
she'd recoup some of that from the mortgage-interest deduction
on her taxes. But remember my rule that there are two sides of
the interest rate: earning and paying. Jennifer (like you) is much
better off on the earning side. For that reason, she should pay cash
for her home. A mortgage at her age isn't a good bet.

True, people often justify a mortgage because buying gets
you better-quality housing than renting, since landlords generally don't maintain housing quality. But wanting better-
quality housing is an argument about consumption, not investment. Consume only what you can pay for. If you want better
housing for the money, buy a less expensive house, one with a
mortgage that you can pay off in two to seven years. Peg your

housing budget to your annual income; that'll give you your target neighborhood and lifestyle.

There is one argument for taking out a mortgage, though it's rarely valid in reality. If you buy when the housing market is heating up, so that the value of your property appreciates at a greater rate than your mortgage-interest rate, then it's a small win. The problem is, no housing market will stay hot over the length of a typical mortgage. And there's always risk involved in buying housing; a market downturn could happen. Paying off the bank, however, is a sure thing.

> Don't buy the worst house in the nicest neighborhood. You may try to catch up with your neighbors by spending more than you can afford.

The bottom line: Jennifer should pay cash for the house, keeping the interest she would have paid the bank for herself, and she should hold down yearly housing expenses to less than a quarter of her income. If she lives in a market with such high home prices that buying a $180,000 home for cash isn't a possibility, it's better for Jennifer to keep renting.

Now we turn to Paul, our widowed salesman (page 43). He's healthy, frugal, and a DIY type, but he's also amassed no savings. His chief asset, really his only one, is the house he inherited from his wife. So shouldn't he sell it? He could invest the proceeds, and isn't that a good thing given his precarious financial state?

Actually, no. Paul needs a place to live, and remember, the house is paid off. That doesn't mean he lives absolutely free; there are property taxes and insurance to pay. But no rental on the market costs as little as those two monthly expenses, so Paul should stay put. A better idea is for him to take in a renter, turning his house into a source of income and a way to pay for a new furnace and other maintenance costs.

By now we've covered several steps to taking control of your retirement plans. I've discussed how to put your best foot forward in the working world, how to spend responsibly and save more, and how to invest and allocate your funds. Many retirement books would stop here. But there's one more important step to go, and this step might pay off the most in ensuring a comfortable retirement for yourself and for others as well, such as your family and neighbors.

Chapter Six:

Voting and Civic Involvement.

Or, we can't get out of this mess one by one.

n the previous chapters, I focused almost exclusively on what you can do as a consumer, investor, saver, and worker to minimize the insecurity you may feel about your retirement. I laid out strategies that will allow you to grow old on your terms. But you need to use one more powerful tool: your role as a member of society who can vote and mobilize voters and residents to support the government programs that ensure a baseline of income and health-care security. If you live to the age of 80, you'll spend as much time being a senior citizen as you did being a child. We need to spend time preparing for this last stage of life. Or, as I like to say, our young selves need to take care of our older selves.

A key part of that is understanding the roles the major government social insurance programs, Social Security and Medicare, will play in your later years. Consider this: They are worth almost half a million dollars to a middle-income American. According to economist Eugene Steuerle and his colleagues at the Urban Institute, a single man who retires in the year 2020 after a full career earning a median wage (about $44,000) can expect to receive $536,000 in Social Security and Medicare benefits. For a married couple, also median earners retiring in 2020, the expected benefits are more than a million dollars. These are stunning numbers. It makes me proud that our country made a commitment during the Depression to make sure that everyone would be protected as they aged. I think you'll agree that most of us wouldn't have the wherewithal to match these amounts, even through a little more financial prudence and picking the right investments.

Despite this valuable insurance, and despite the obvious good these programs do for Americans, they're underappreciated. Social Security in particular is chronically under attack by people who want to privatize it in the name of smaller government. Political elites use it as a bargaining chip in budget negotiations, calling for cuts. (Don't be fooled; raising the normal retirement age to 70 is a benefits cut, however they might dress it up.) But here are the key realities of Social Security that everyone should know:

Reality #1: Social Security is an essential form of insurance. It provides support for young families in the event of the death or disability of its breadwinners. It helps children with severe disabilities. It insures workers against old age, disability, or dying and leaving behind a survivor without adequate income. As a retirement benefit, Social Security is worth about $300,000 for the average household. Equally important, its benefits are guaranteed. In contrast, 401(k) returns are very much *not* guaranteed.

Reality #2: Social Security and Medicare benefit all workers, whether white-, pink-, or blue-collar. In 2012, 55 million Americans (out of a population of 313 million) cashed Social Security checks. These were members of all segments of society—rich and poor, left and right.

Economist Moshe Milevsky makes this clear in his excellent book *Your Money Milestones: A Guide to Making the 9 Most Important Financial Decisions of Your Life.* He writes that all households, rich and poor, have the government as an economic partner. We all pay taxes, and we all receive benefits from it. Through our votes, we exercise some control over how that money is spent. So no matter what your political leanings are or what your tax bracket is, the government is part of your financial life and always will be. This is equally true for the corporate CEO, the small-business owner, and the starving artist.

Reality #3: Social Security is on sound financial footing. In fact, it's a lean and efficient success. In 2015, its administrative expenses (as a percentage of all Social Security spending) were less than 1 percent, falling from 2.2 percent in 1957. Compare that with the average 401(k), which has expenses three times as high!

Any clear-sighted look at Social Security's finances, free of politically motivated spin, shows that the program is in strong shape. It has a reserve fund to pay all benefits until 2031 without any change in current policy. And with some small policy changes—for instance, raising the payroll tax by 2 percentage points or eliminating the earnings cap—we could put the system in balance for the next 75 years. (The earning cap means that only wage income up to a certain ceiling is currently subject to Social Security taxes. In 2015, it was $118,500, but that figure will rise in response to wage inflation.) We are easily poised to keep the system healthy well into the future.

Privatizing Social Security by diverting some of the 12.4 percent payroll tax (divided equally between employers and employees in 2013) would cost the system more as money is diverted from the program. Also, the private accounts are more risky and cost more to manage. Simply put, privatization costs more to deliver less valuable benefits. There's no institution or combination of institutions in the business world that could take in $600 billion a year and get it to America's seniors in the form of checks by the third Wednesday of the month, every month, as Social Security has done since 1940.

In 2013, legislation was introduced to expand Social Security; I testified in the Senate subcommittee hearings. That was the first time advocates for the system had gone on the offensive since the 1970s, and it was a testament to Social Security's importance and strength. Although no legislation was passed at that time, you're going to keep hearing about this issue. Both parties understand that Social Security is foremost in voters' concerns.

An expansion is within reach, since far from being set in stone, the system is designed for continuous improvement. There are many ways to increase Social Security benefits and many easy ways to pay for an expansion. In early 2014, after a seminar in New Orleans, a financial planner

> There are easy ways to raise revenues in order to maintain and expand Social Security benefits.

(a Republican) told me that assuring Social Security's future is easy: We just have to eliminate the earnings cap like Medicare has done and the system will be funded indefinitely. We could also use the Consumer Price Index for the Elderly, which is a more generous measure of inflation, as it takes the rising costs of health care into account.

I think I've made it clear that worry about Social Security's finances is completely unfounded: The program is perfectly instituted to solve a looming problem for the nation. In contrast, 401(k) plans are woefully underfunded. In 2010, 75 percent of workers nearing retirement had less than $30,000 in their 401(k). Sixty percent of low-income households are at risk of being unable to maintain their already-modest standard of living in retirement.

Individual savings don't look much better. About a third of households don't have any savings at all. More than 40 percent wouldn't have enough to cover basic expenses if they lost their main source of income. For this reason, many workers are tapping into their 401(k) plans early. In the years after the great recession of 2007 to 2009, employees were taking out about 40 cents from their retirement accounts for every dollar going in. Their 401(k) plans and IRAs were being used as piggy banks to an alarming extent, when these accounts had been created with the opposite vision. Instead of being withdrawn before retirement, their funds were supposed to be the foundation of a financially secure old age.

With personal savings in such poor shape, Social Security has become the linchpin of many Americans' retirement. Today, Social Security provides 37 percent of income for the average American over 65, and about 80 to 90 percent of income for seniors in the bottom half of income distribution. Given the state of private pensions, this situation isn't likely to change anytime soon; in fact, it's more likely that the standard of living for seniors will fall, and more middle-class workers will be downwardly mobile, becoming poor and near-poor retirees.

The upshot: If there is a "problem" with Social Security, it's this: It's not generous enough to counteract the sorry state of retirement savings nationwide. The debate over Social Security is upside down—we need to make Social Security much more generous. And that's completely possible. We have the money to help everyone save for retirement.

As long as we have an effective democracy, the public will resist cutting Social Security, because the program works extraordinarily well. Social Security has been wildly successful at raising living standards for the elderly, even as other forms of retirement savings have grown shakier. Social Security is not a problem to be solved; it is the foundation of American retirement security. Along with, of course, Medicare.

The value of Medicare

Along with Social Security, the most successful social policy in America in the last 100 years has been Medicare. Americans from every walk of life, political persuasion, and income level are enrolled in this program and use it to get health care. Together these programs allow everyone, not just the rich, to live a normal human life span and have a period of rest and freedom at the end of their working lives. (By the way, Social Security and Medicare are two of the main reasons many people over age 65 are living longer—income and health care have that effect.) In old age everyone has the same health insurance policy—finally! Medicare is the great leveler.

A little more about Medicare: It's an astonishingly efficient way to provide health care. One criticism of the program is that it's too big, and therefore inefficient. But in many ways, Medicare's size is its strength. For example, its scale allows it to analyze vast amounts of information to discern which medical practices are good ones and which are ineffective. Based on that research, Medicare can bring the best care to elderly patients. In the 1990s, Medicare funded mammography because mammography lowers breast cancer mortality rates. More recently, in 2006, Medicare acted to bring the best obesity surgery to all patients regardless of which state they lived in.

The second-best use of Medicare's size, and thus power, is its ability to negotiate with the best health-care providers and hospitals to give patients the lowest fees. There's one unfortunate exception to this: Congress has specifically legislated that Medicare cannot negotiate special deals with the pharmaceutical industry. So put this in your tickler file: The next time anyone tells you that Medicare is too expensive, politely agree, and then recruit them to lobby Congress to give Medicare the ability to negotiate the cost of drugs. That would certainly lower the cost of Medicare. If you don't believe it, look at Canada. There, because of government negotiations, pharmaceuticals cost a fraction of what they cost in the United States.

> **Congress should give Medicare the ability to negotiate the best prices for pharmaceuticals.**

It's also crucial that we protect Medicare from another looming threat: the threat that Congress will reduce reimbursement rates to a point so low that physicians will leave the system and Medicare patients' choices will be restricted. We need to support farsighted politicians who won't let this happen.

Worried about costs? Medicare's administrative costs are a fraction of what private insurance companies spend. Consider: Medicare's overhead is less than 2 percent, and Medicare Advantage plans (plans in which private companies contract with Medicare to provide benefits) have an overhead of 14 percent. In contrast, the Affordable Care Act currently limits (limits!) insurance overhead to 20 percent.

How does Medicare keep costs down to less than 2 percent? It takes advantage of its national scope and overwhelming size, and most important, the government doesn't have to pay shareholders dividends from profit. Private health insurers enjoy higher profit rates than all other industries and their CEOs. According to *Fortune* magazine, five of the ten highest-paid CEOs in 2013 were in health care. Only one in the top ten was from Big Oil, the industry that many Americans would associate with rampant profiteering.

But it's not just Social Security and Medicare that citizens need to get behind. It's Medicaid as well.

Medicaid? Wait, that one really is for poor people, isn't it?

No, in truth, Medicaid helps middle-income senior citizens as much as or more than working-class seniors. The poor qualify more often for Medicaid, but they receive only an average of $2,200 from it, whereas the middle-class elderly get an average of $3,300. The reason? Middle-income people live longer. A middle-class male in bad health at age 70 has about 7.1 years to live. A low-income man in good health can expect to live the same 7.1 years. Poverty undermines health. The middle-income retiree lives longer, thus collecting benefits longer.

Consider the case of Bill and Betty. This middle-class couple retired, outlived the lump sum from their IRA, and were getting along on Social Security. Bill had Alzheimer's, but Betty was able to look after him—until she came home from the doctor one day with very bad news. She was in hospice and dead from lung cancer within 17 weeks. But before that happened, Betty and her family put Bill in a good nursing home, paying for one month with the remainder of what was in the couple's checking and savings accounts. After that, Medicaid took over.

Medicaid and Social Security were invaluable to Bill and Betty. Some people would have you believe that being middle income, plus having a modicum of financial good sense, is a failsafe against financial hard times late in life. But that's not always true, and for perfectly good reasons. As I've already pointed out, estimating your own life expectancy is difficult (not to mention unpleasantly morbid). So is speculating about the nature and length of illnesses that might befall you or your spouse. Social Security, Medicare, and yes, Medicaid, are saviors for the many people for whom the DIY retirement-planning model is not enough.

A glimpse into the future

Congress has been slow to acknowledge that the DIY retirement system has been a disaster for the average American. But there are people taking up the cause, including me. My proposal is a supplement to Social Security called a Guaranteed Retirement Account (GRA). Noted in *The New York Times* as one of the most innovative economic ideas of 2008, the GRA would be a national pension system that would remedy the failures of the 401(k) and IRA model—in fact, for most people it would replace the 401(k) and IRA—and would help everyone accumulate a solid nest egg for retirement. This is how it would work:

1. Every employee would contribute 2.5 percent of pay via an automatic paycheck deduction—in addition to Social Security contributions—and every employer would match the amount, raising the total contribution to 5 percent of annual pay before taxes. If you earn an annual salary of $50,000, you and your company would both put in $1,250 per year. As with a 401(k), you could check your balance any time you wished, watching the interest accrue.

2. Congress would provide a refundable tax credit—meaning people who don't have to pay any taxes would still get a cash refund that went into their retirement account—of

$600 for every worker to offset their contribution on April 15 or before. I advocate a tax credit instead of a tax deduction because a deduction would favor top earners—as it does under the current system. The tax breaks for retirement savings give more help (proportionally) to higher-income taxpayers than those in the working and middle class. Famously, 2012 presidential election disclosures revealed that Mitt Romney had between $21 million and $102 million in a tax-advantaged Roth IRA. (That's a wide spectrum, but campaign rules require candidates to report only a range, not a figure.) Giving tax breaks to a man of Romney's net worth just isn't a good use of taxpayer funds. President Obama, in 2015, announced his intention to close this loophole. But the GRA's tax credit would give $600 to everyone, which especially lightens the burden on low-wage workers. (There's no extra cost to the Treasury. The switch from a deduction to a refundable tax credit would be revenue neutral.) In fact, it would entirely cover the contribution of someone making minimum wage.

3. The Social Security Administration would collect the funds, and then professional fiduciaries would invest the money in low-risk, low-fee funds.

4. This plan would guarantee a 3 percent rate of return adjusted for inflation. Although this might sound low compared with the S&P's average annual performance in recent years, it is consistent with long-term economic growth. And remember, under my plan this rate of return would be guaranteed, even though during some years the S&P is certain to dip into negative territory. In years when the market is booming, the trustees could raise the rate of return, or they could put the higher earnings into a rainy-day fund.

5. No one would be able to take withdrawals before retirement, except in case of permanent disability or death, in which case survivors would receive benefits.

6. You could begin taking benefits at the minimum Social Security retirement age, although you could choose to keep working longer, thus increasing your balance and your eventual annuity. No one would be penalized for working later in life; in fact, the GRA would encourage work, since delaying retirement would cause your balance to grow.

7. The GRA would pay benefits as an inflation-adjusted annuity, not a lump sum, eliminating the risk of outliving benefits. What *inflation-adjusted* means is that if inflation is running at 2 percent, the interest you earn would be 2 percent above that earnings. Your benefit would be based on your contributions and the investment income earned over your lifetime.

8. The GRA would provide some choices at payout. Though most of the money would come as a monthly check, as a pension does, you'd have the option (at retirement age, not early) to take a 10 percent lump-sum withdrawal in exchange for a smaller annuity. That is, if you took the lump-sum payment, your monthly benefit would decrease. Alternatively, you could choose to get a smaller monthly check to leave a death benefit for a survivor. (That might be attractive to people who have reason to believe their life expectancy is shorter than average.)

Under this plan, a full-time worker who retires at age 65 after working 40 years would get a benefit equal to approximately 30 percent of pre-retirement income. Since Social Security will provide roughly 40 percent, this person would retire on 70 percent of his pre-retirement income—the percentage I told you to keep in mind way back in Chapter Two.

I think you can see how a GRA incorporates the best aspects of both pensions and 401(k) plans—and more to the point, remedies the failings of 401(k) plans and IRAs. Under my plan, individuals couldn't forget or fail to put away money toward retirement, nor could employers opt out of providing a match. High management fees couldn't erode savings, because the money would go into a large pooled fund managed by a not-for-profit trusteeship. Unsophisticated or overwhelmed individuals wouldn't put their money in the hands of "Guys" who are largely salesmen paid on commission, nor would they choose investments based on advertisements on late-night television. Nor could they load up on company stock, thereby failing to diversify their investments, which can be a problem with 401(k) plans. They also couldn't break into their accounts to pay for non-retirement expenses.

> People should be able to save in add-on Social Security accounts that are protected from high fees and unsophisticated investments.

I laid out my idea for the Guaranteed Retirement Account in an earlier book, *When I'm Sixty-Four: The Plot Against Pensions and the Plan to Save Them*. Because of the shorter length and different focus of this book, I've given a shorter explanation here. But if you're interested enough, you can get more details in *Sixty-Four*.

STATES LEAD THE WAY

How far off is a Guaranteed Retirement Account? A decade? More? Certainly it'll be an uphill battle. The chief beneficiaries of the rise of the 401(k) and the IRA have been banks and brokers, and they would have a lot to lose from a changeover to a GRA plan. You can see how a switch to a national retirement plan would have the whole financial sector reaching for antacids. And as I've said, they have armies of lobbyists with which to fight such a plan.

But some states aren't waiting for change to come from the federal government. In 2012, California became the first state to pass a version of a Guaranteed Retirement plan called a Secure Choice Retirement Plan. The name doesn't matter; the basic idea does. Under the California plan, all private-sector employers will be required to deduct a percentage of workers' income and put the money into a retirement account. The plan will also cover the few public employees who aren't covered at work. Professional fiduciaries, probably the same managers who invest money for CALPERS, the pension fund for state public employees, will manage the account. Unlike a Guaranteed Retirement plan, employees will be able to opt out of Secure Choice, but otherwise, the program works essentially like a pension, and the quality of the money management will be vastly superior to the average 401(k) or IRA. The bottom line is that when Secure Choice is up and running, all working Californians will have access to a safe, secure investment vehicle for their retirement savings.

Other states—Oregon, Maryland, Connecticut, Illinois, and Washington—are considering similar plans. This is an encouraging sign. Though I advocate for a national plan, I've called for states to mandate employees to have an advance-funded retirement account if the federal government doesn't pass a GRA plan.

But maybe, despite all the advantages, you don't like the feel of Guaranteed Retirement Accounts because it seems like "forced" savings; there would be no individual choice in investments, and you couldn't get at the money before retirement (except in the case of permanent disability). In my plan, as in Social Security, no one can opt out (although under most proposals under consideration at the state level, there is an opt-out clause).

Or your objection could be simpler. You might be saying, "Why should I trust the government to manage my money?"

Believe me, these are arguments I've heard before, as has anyone else who promotes a universal supplement to Social Security. Let me address the second one first. The government will not manage your money. In the GRA plan, the government collects the contributions and then chooses the best private money managers to invest them. An added benefit here is that because of the huge amount of money being invested, these professionals would have the clout to demand the best deals.

And about a GRA plan being mandatory savings, with no early withdrawals or individual control over investments? Consider this: We've already tried a system in which we choose whether and how much money to put in our retirement accounts, what to invest that money in, and whether to withdraw it early for needs other than retirement or disability. That national experiment is the 401(k) system, and I've clearly pointed out the results: Most workers have saved less than $30,000 toward retirement, when what they need is close to $1 million.

I'm not blaming the victim. It would have been hard to manage a personal pension account in the best economic times, and these have not been the best. My point is that most of us are simply not equipped to be pension-fund managers for a pension plan of one. In a perfect world, we wouldn't need Guaranteed Retirement Accounts, because every employee would act like a human spreadsheet and contribute adequately to a 401(k), every employer would match funds, and all the money would go into low-risk, low-fee investments.

But we don't live in a spreadsheet world. It's hard to put money aside during hard times. And harder yet to resist breaking into a nest egg during those hard times. Yet we gladly pay for insurance of various kinds because we know we can't predict or control the misfortunes that might befall us. This is why Social Security is so popular. We like well-designed programs that help when needed, in times of disability, retirement, or death. I propose the GRA as a supplement to Social Security's base—a savings plan that is easy, secure, and pays out a steady, guaranteed stream of income during retirement.

A change like this can start very simply, and at a grassroots level. It has before. In 1933, two years before the president promoted and Congress enacted Social Security, an activist physician named Francis Townsend published a letter to the editor of the *Long Beach Press-Telegram* in Long Beach, California, calling for a simple taxpayer-funded plan to end misery among the elderly. Townsend's plan advocated for the government to pay $100 monthly for everyone over 65. This call to action, to get money in the hands of seniors immediately, triggered determined elders to form the "Townsend Plan." The movement was so strong that within a few years 20 states had enacted, or threatened to enact, old-age-security programs. The federal government stepped in to avoid a patchwork of mismatched state plans.

The movement we need now is for the plan I called for in 2008, Guaranteed Retirement Accounts. The GRA plan would have every worker (or workers or employer, depending on the legal status of the plan) pay at least 5 percent into an individual account, invested professionally in a fund—a national pension fund. The account would earn the highest risk-adjusted returns at the lowest possible fees and be redeemed to supplement a Social Security retiree or survivor benefit. That would be that. I've showed that if every worker saved 17 to 20 percent of their paycheck, they would have enough retirement income after a lifetime of work. The GRA plan calls for a 5 percent contribution that would be added to the 12.8 percent FICA tax we (and our employer) pay for regular Social Security. We automatically save 17.8 percent of every paycheck, and we're set. An elegant solution to our upcoming retirement crisis.

How do we get there from here? Let's pull out our pencils, pens, and iPads and start another movement like we did in 1933. Consider it a "Back to the Future" movement, lest we go back to a future of 50 percent poverty rates among the elderly and old people forced to move in with their adult children or to poorhouses, before Social Security was instituted.

HOW YOU CAN HELP

When I was 21 and working on my dissertation at UC–Berkeley, I was asked to speak about changes to Social Security to an organization called the Gray Panthers and their radical cousin, the Older Women's League (OWL). But as it turned out, I probably learned as much from these dignified and confident women as they did from me. I'll never forget the lesson they taught me: Know the details of the government programs that you pay for, know what is in your self-interest, and teach others the importance of voting. They knew that a secure old age isn't just a matter of individual pennies in individual piggy banks: The big picture matters.

It still does. Public policy has a direct effect on the quality of our lives. What Congress does—or what we make Congress do—will affect you in your old age. So stay informed. Understand what's being discussed and planned in Washington for Social Security, Medicare, and Medicaid. And keep voting. Politicians who understand the value of these government programs need your support—as do those lawmakers who see the need for a national pension system like the GRA. In fact, if you're so inspired, go beyond voting to political activism, like the Gray Panthers and OWL members who impressed me so much.

Future taxpayers will thank you, the good people serving the overcrowded homeless shelters will thank you for not adding to the line when you don't get in line, and your adult children will thank you. Most poignantly, your older self will thank you—so take care of that person.

Appendix:

Further Resources

ooking for more information on the subjects we've covered, or just some interesting reads? Many of these websites and books are ones I've mentioned earlier in the book, but here they are rounded up in one place, for convenience's sake.

Websites

aarp.org

I know: You're not retired yet; you're still young and vital! But if you can ignore the pop-up ads for walk-in bathtubs, this site is a treasure trove of information. It includes the retirement-planning calculator I mentioned in Chapter Two, a Social Security benefits calculator, job hunting tips, news from Washington, D.C., on issues affecting retirement, and more. Even if you're still under 55 and in the middle of your working life, this site can help you with your retirement planning. Besides, how stodgy can the AARP be? They have a Twitter feed!

moneyover55.about.com

This is the blog of Dana Anspach, a very knowledgeable fee-only financial planner. I'm happy to recommend her very clear and honest articles. If you like what you read on About.com, she's also on Facebook and Twitter.

wiseradvisor.com
If you're sold on the idea of a fee-only financial planner, this is a good place to find one.

dinkytown.net
My friend Jodi Compton, the novelist, advises me that the site takes its odd name from a neighborhood in Minneapolis. But had dinkytown.net been taken, they could've named this site Calculator Heaven. Of particular interest is a page under "Investments" named "Compare Investment Fees." It'll make starkly clear how much a mutual fund with a 2 percent fee structure will cost you compared with an index fund that charges .1 percent. One caveat: Be sure you understand what each calculator is estimating for you and that your underlying assumptions (such as how much money you can contribute to an account or the rate of return you'll make) are realistic. A calculator is only as good as the numbers you provide it.

Books and articles

Pound Foolish: Exposing the Dark Side of the Personal Finance Industry, by Helaine Olen. This is an excellent exposé of an industry that seems like it's the average investor's best friend but is often his or her worst enemy.

Your Money Milestones: A Guide to Making the 9 Most Important Financial Decisions of Your Life, by Moshe Milevsky. Milevsky, a university professor with a background in both math and finance, discusses the big money-related choices you're likely to face, including incurring student loans, buying a home (or not), and when to retire.

Never Say Die: The Myth and Marketing of the New Old Age, by Susan Jacoby. America is a society with an ever-growing life expectancy and a huge generation (the baby boomers) about to cross over from retirement age to old age. Jacoby's book is a clear-sighted look at what it means to grow old in America and at how realistic the idea that "age is nothing but a number" truly is (or rather, isn't). Eye opening, but not for the faint of heart.

Falling Short: The Coming Retirement Crisis and What to Do About It, by Charles D. Ellis, Alicia H. Munnell, and Andrew D. Eschtruth. This is a nice, short book on retirement policy from Oxford University Press.

Get What's Yours: The Secrets to Maxing Out Your Social Security, by Laurence J. Kotlikoff, Philip Moeller, and Paul Solman. This book teaches you how to exploit a loophole in Social Security that Congress should loose as soon as possible.

"Your 401(k) Is Out to Get You," by James Kwak, *The Atlantic* magazine. If I haven't sold you on the idea that the 401(k) has been bad for the average American, let James Kwak have a shot at it. Kwak makes many of the points I've covered—that 401(k) plans lead to inadequate saving, early withdrawals, and high fees. But he also draws special attention to the way members of the asset-management industry push their own poorly performing funds on 401(k) plan participants, who don't know enough to get out of them and into better-performing funds. Find the article here: theatlantic.com/business/archive/2013/03 /your-401-k-is-out-to-get-you/274408/.

(Please note that the links to these online articles were good at time of publication, but I can't guarantee how long they'll be valid.)

Index

D

E

F

About the author

Teresa Ghilarducci is the Bernard L. and Irene Schwartz professor of economics at The New School for Social Research. She has a PhD in economics from the University of California at Berkeley and has taught previously at the University of Notre Dame. Her 2008 book, *When I'm Sixty-Four: The Plot Against Pensions and the Plan to Save Them*, was named as containing the best economic idea of 2008 by *The New York Times*. Her book *Labor's Capital: The Politics and Economics of Private Pensions* won the American Publishers award for the best business book of 1992. She has written articles for or been interviewed by *Time*, *U.S. News and World Report*, *The New York Times*, *Parade* magazine, *Money*, and *Kiplinger's*, among others. Her website can be found at teresaghilarducci.org.

Notes and Calculations

Notes and Calculations

Notes and Calculations